Post-Continental Voices

Selected Interviews

First published by Zero Books, 2010
Zero Books is an imprint of John Hunt Publishing Ltd., Laurel House, Station Approach,
Alresford, Hants, SO24 9JH, UK
office1@o-books.net
www.o-books.com

For distributor details and how to order please visit the 'Ordering' section on our website.

Text copyright: Paul John Ennis 2009

ISBN: 978 1 84694 385 0

A CIP catalogue record for this book is available from the British Library.

Design: Tom Davies

Printed in the UK by CPI Antony Rowe
Printed in the USA by Offset Paperback Mfrs, Inc

O Books operates a distinctive and ethical publishing philosophy in
all areas of our business, from our global network of authors to
production and worldwide distribution.

Post-Continental Voices

Selected Interviews

Edited by Paul John Ennis

Winchester, UK
Washington, USA

CONTENTS

Introduction by Paul John Ennis   1

1. Interview with Graham Harman   6
2. Interview with Jeffrey Malpas   19
3. Interview with Stuart Elden   35
4. Interview with Ian Bogost   48
5. Interview with Levi R. Bryant   64
6. Interview with Adrian Ivakhiv   83
7. Interview with Lee Braver   98

Introduction

In the following interviews each thinker is asked about their academic development, their hopes for post-Continental philosophy, and whether they can provide some advice for aspiring academic philosophers. They have been picked for their achievements, popularity and potential but I've also tried to choose people known for their kindness in helping out a graduate student or two. This collection of interviews can be read as an advice handbook or an introduction to post-Continental philosophy. Either way the point is to provide the reader with a small push on the winding stairs up to the ivory tower. The seven thinkers involved are a mix of the familiar and the unfamiliar. There are established names but also a couple of surprises.

Despite pointing to something beyond Continental philosophy these thinkers all retain an affinity to that tradition. There is a profound engagement here with Continental philosophy especially with the phenomenologist Martin Heidegger. Some of the best practical advice contained in these pages pertains to reading phenomenology. What is striking is how these thinkers bring phenomenology into the twenty-first century. It is a peculiar product of the twenty first century that brought these interviews together. These interviews first appeared on my blog in early 2009. The idea was simple: could I convince established academics to give us an insight into the academic scene today? My hope was that we would trash out some basic issues but those involved went above and beyond my rather limited hopes.

Academic philosophers, especially successful ones, can sometimes look like they sprang from the ether fully formed aged thirty-five, tenured and with a number of book contracts. What these interviews reveal is that the path to academia is a tough slog and that slog does not necessarily end with a job offer. It is a good thing then to remind ourselves why we have entered such a difficult, and all too often absurd, field. Hopefully these interviews provide some answers and with an increasingly difficult job market that reminder is more important than ever. The interviews certainly give us a taste of how difficult things can be but one cannot overlook how enthusiastic these thinkers remain about their subject matter after all these years. It is this enthusiasm which was ultimately the deciding factor when making my choices. There is no denying that the selection process is somewhat arbitrary. I did not collate how many times they had been referenced in footnotes or whether they had just published something that needed some publicity. Rather I tried to think who I wanted to read myself and then whether that desire might extend to other people. After asking around I then settled on the thinkers presented in these pages. I hope that this method is not too biased and that whatever bias can be discerned is so strikingly obvious that nobody can take my biases seriously.

Where my *real* bias will become clear is with the questions. There is a heavy emphasis in the questions on Heidegger. Heidegger is my access point to philosophy, the subject of my dissertation and by extension the people I read tend also to have read Heidegger. Readers who simply cannot stand Heidegger are asked to skip past our ontological musings and onto the other questions. Heideggerians are warned that the Heidegger presented in these pages tends to be a radically new and unfamiliar one. With that proviso in mind let us introduce our thinkers.

Our first interview is with Graham Harman. Harman will be familiar to those working in Continental philosophy for his radical re-reading of Heidegger (*Tool-Being: Heidegger and the Metaphysics of Objects,* 2002 and *Heidegger Explained: from Phenomenon to Thing,* 2007). This has led to the development of his own "object-oriented philosophy" within the umbrella movement of speculative realism (the other speculative realists are Iain Hamilton Grant, Ray Brassier, and Quentin Meillassoux). This reinterpretation of Heidegger has broadened out into a form of "guerrilla metaphysics" (*Guerrilla Metaphysics: Phenomenology and the Carpentry of Things*, 2005 and *Prince of Networks: Bruno Latour and Metaphysics*, 2009). Harman's work is known for its clear, unassuming style as well as his attempts to revive neglected metaphysical positions.

We then move onto Jeffrey Malpas. Malpas is well known for his work on place and philosophical topography (*Place and Experience: A Philosophical Topography*, 1999). He has instigated an entire new direction in Heidegger scholarship (*Heidegger's Topology: Being, Place, World*, 2007). Malpas has been slowly pushing philosophical topography into increasingly interesting areas exploring the problematic nexus of rootedness, ethics, and the politics of place. For Malpas, the question is never simply what is the concept of place but how does the concept of place infiltrate, affect or distort one's identity or sense of self. In this interview we get closer to understanding why place has played such an important part in Malpas's career and in particular how he managed to stick to his guns and pursue a relatively undeveloped issue in philosophy.

With Stuart Elden we meet our first non-philosopher. A geographer by trade, Elden has managed to write some of the most interesting work in Continental philosophy in the past decade without actually belonging to a philosophy department (*Understanding Henri Lefebvre: Theory and the Possible*, 2004 and *Speaking Against Number: Heidegger, Language and the Politics of Calculation*, 2006). Elden is perhaps the post-Continental philosopher *par excellence* applying Continental thinkers to issues of globalization, sovereignty and territory. With Elden Continental philosophers are directly challenged, shaken up and whatever remains serviceable is put to damn good use (*Mapping the Present: Heidegger, Foucault and the project of a spatial history*, 2001).

Ian Bogost is our second non-philosopher. Bogost is a videogame theorist and game-designer. Bogost treats videogames seriously and has no problem treating Derrida, Deleuze, and others on the same plane as *Grand Theft Auto*, *The Sims* and *Half-Life* (see *Unit Operations: an Approach to Videogame Criticism*, 2006 and *Racing the Beam: the Atari Video Computer System*, 2009). In his interview Bogost charts one of the most unlikely career trajectories imaginable and one that should offer hope to those with not quite traditional research interests. It is Bogost's thesis that videogames are not only interesting as media or structures but that they can be used to put forward arguments (*Persuasive Games: The Expressive Power of Videogames*, 2007).

Levi R. Bryant is an emerging thinker and the scope of his ambition is clear. Bryant wants nothing less than to develop a new ontology. Reading Bryant involves a lot of theoretical work and it is not uncommon to encounter unremittingly complex discussions of Deleuze, Badiou, or Žižek (*Difference and Givenness: Deleuze's Transcendental Empiricism and the Ontology of Immanence*, 2008). Nonetheless attentive readers will find that with a little bit of patience Bryant is fusing together his own brand of post-metaphysics and one that never averts its gaze from the possibilities for social or political engagement. With a previous foray as a psychoanalyst Bryant infuses his work with a Lacanian twist – a twist that crops up in our interview and helps explain a thing or two about Continental philosophy.

Adrian Ivakhiv gives us an insight into the most recognizable form of political philosophy to have emerged in recent years: environmental philosophy. Ivakhiv runs the gamut of post-Continental themes from issues of space and place, the intersections of phenomenological thinking and ecology (eco-phenomenology) and problems of identity formation (*Claiming Sacred Ground: Pilgrims and Politics at Glastonbury and Sedona*, 2001). It is in thinkers such as Ivakhiv that we can discover a certain post-Continental *attitude*. Ivakhiv gives us an insight into how philosophy looks not as a critical discipline but as a discipline that may need to be critiqued. With Ivakhiv we get a clear indication that the division between philosophy and other disciplines will eventually give way and will do so because the academics of the future are no longer satisfied with the boundaries they have been bequeathed.

We end our series of interviews with Lee Braver. Braver gives an important analysis of the Analytic-Continental divide, positing that they are both, at heart, dealing with the same problem: realism versus anti-realism (*A Thing of the World: A History of Continental Anti-Realism*, 2007). It is this focus on realism and anti-realism that makes Braver such an important writer and he is rightly known for his ability to explain difficult ideas clearly (*Heidegger's Later Writings: A Reader's Guide*, 2009). A safe hand when explicating either Wittgenstein or Heidegger, he gives a good insight into what post-Continental philosophy might become. In his typically clear style Braver guides us through his experience engaging with both traditions and like Ivakhiv suggests that the divide cannot hold for much longer. Braver brings us back to a central issue in post-Continental thinking: dialogue.

With that spirit of dialogue in mind let us begin the interviews.

Paul John Ennis,
University College Dublin, 2009.
ennis.paul@gmail.com

Interview with Graham Harman

Paul John Ennis: You've stated before that you have read the entire Heidegger Gesamtausgabe (Collected Works) *and yet you managed to write a book called* Heidegger Explained *that is less than two hundred pages. Do you think there is a tendency among academic philosophers to mystify Heidegger?*

Graham Harman: There is certainly a tendency to make him too complicated. As a group, great philosophers of Heidegger's magnitude are not primarily motivated to catalogue all the fascinating concrete details in the world. That impulse can of course be found in zoology, botany, linguistics, anthropology, and other such fields. By contrast, philosophers tend to be great systematizers, which means great simplifiers as well. In my view, to understand a philosophy means to grasp a handful of basic intuitions from which the entire philosophy unfolds. This true simplicity of a philosophy can take years of hard work to discover, but it remains the goal of interpretation. Heidegger suggests this method himself with his famous maxim: "every great thinker has one great thought." I think that's a slight exaggeration; it's more like two or three great thoughts. But the basic point is correct.

Since Heidegger was such a prolific writer, though not a prolific publisher of what he wrote, there is plenty of lush jungle for Heidegger specialists to study. But it's fairly repetitive jungle. There's no shame in that – that's what first philosophers do, as opposed to zoologists, botanists, linguists, and anthropologists. We are specialists in the simplicity of things, and hence we constantly repeat ourselves in one way or another. But of course the world isn't altogether simple, and that's why philosophers are not masters of all the other disciplines, just as we are not their handmaids.

One of the benefits of having read the entire *Gesamtausgabe*, and indeed one of my motives for having done so, is that now I cannot be bluffed with obscure references by specialists who might wring their hands over how complicated he is, and how many years of labor it takes even to understand *Being and Time*. I've already put in those years of labor, and have earned the right to say that Heidegger is actually pretty simple.

Paul John Ennis: Can you tell us a little about your reasons for writing your dissertation on Heidegger and how you came to place the tool-analysis at the heart of his thinking?

Graham Harman: The story began some years before the dissertation itself. Many high school students in Iowa earn money in the summer by detasseling corn. This involves walking down several miles worth of rows and pulling the fuzzy tassels out of the plants to prevent unwanted cross-pollination. It's horrible work in muddy, hot, mosquito-infested fields. Despite the heat you have to wear long sleeves or else your arms are covered with pesticide and a rash breaks out. But you earn a good summer income by the standards of high school students, and the detasseling period only lasts for a couple of weeks at most.

The relevance of this is that I bought my first copy of *Being and Time* with a corn detasseling paycheck, between my junior and senior years of high school. But I struggled with *Being and Time*, and quickly ended my first three attempts to read it. I couldn't really get a foothold in what the question of the meaning of being was about.

Then something happened during my sophomore year in college. I was at St. John's in Annapolis, which has as classical a curriculum as one can find. We had a class one day about medieval logic. For various reasons I found the discussion frustrating, and felt more confused than ever about the topic. After class I went straight to the college bookstore and bought Heidegger's *Metaphysical Foundations of Logic*, hoping it might help. It turned out to be life-changing book. Though it didn't teach me much about logic, it did open my way into Heidegger's thinking for the first time. Immediately after reading it, I returned to *Being and Time*, was able to finish the whole book in a month, and finally felt that it made sense. Over the course of the next half-year I read everything the college library had by Heidegger in English, which was something like eleven books. The library also had his complete works in German, too. But I'd been a bit lazy during my four years of high school German, and found Heidegger in the original too difficult at that point. I remember thinking: "I'll never be able to do this."

What first made me serious about reading the German volumes was the publication in 1989 of Heidegger's *Beiträge zur Philosophie*, which everyone was celebrating as his second *magnum opus*. I now view that claim as wildly exaggerated, but at the time, that was the word on the street. I didn't want to be deprived of the supposed second major work, but it was obviously going to take years to translate the *Beiträge* into English. So eventually I bought a copy of the German, and forced myself to read it and to look up every single word I didn't know. This took a very long time: more than a year, in fact. But it turned out to be an excellent starting point. Learning Heidegger's German from the *Beiträge* is like exercising with ankle weights: it's making things tougher than they usually are, and this makes you stronger. None of the other volumes are as hard to read as that one, especially since like all authors Heidegger uses a fairly limited range of vocabulary that is easily mastered with practice. The second volume I read in German was the famous 1929/30 course on boredom and animal life (the English was not yet available). I took it to a café, unhappy that I had no dictionary with me, but before I knew it I had blazed through seventy-five pages without a dictionary in just a few hours, and that was when I realized it would be pretty easy to read a whole bunch of the volumes.

A close friend then asked why I simply didn't read them all, and inspired by that question, I embarked on the great "Manhattan Project" of my twenties, finishing the entire set shortly after my thirtieth birthday. It's one of those things I've never regretted doing, because I'm still convinced there was no greater philosopher in the twentieth century than Heidegger, and no better way to orient your own thinking than with a thorough top-to-bottom survey of his thought. From the ages of nineteen to twenty-nine, I was convinced that he was basically right about all philosophical issues other than the obvious political ones, so any criticisms I make of Heidegger are not those of an outsider whose whole purpose is to criticize.

I know that's a long prologue to get to the question about my dissertation. But perhaps now you'll see that by dissertation stage, the choice of Heidegger as a topic was inevitable. I did toy with a few alternatives, but it was just that: toying. It really had to be Heidegger, since he was my point of entry into serious philosophy.

You also ask how I came to place the tool-analysis at the center of my reading. That stems from 1991 and 1992, during my first two years of graduate school. I'd always liked the tool-analysis, as everyone does, but it gradually occurred to me that there wasn't really anything else going on in Heidegger aside from this interplay of shadow and light, or veiled and unveiled, which takes on far more concrete form in the tool-analysis than anywhere else in his works. I thought I had found Heidegger's "one great thought" at last, and I still think that's the case.

Incidentally, I was not yet a "realist" at that stage. I was still the usual sort of agnostic about the outer world that most people from a phenomenological background tend to be. Only in 1997 (entertainingly enough, it happened on Christmas morning) did I extend the tool-analysis to cover inanimate interactions as well. That was mostly under Whitehead's influence, since I didn't read a word of Latour until a few months later.

Paul John Ennis: You talk a lot about the tool-analysis in your work on Heidegger, placing it at the center of his thinking. To what extent have you rejected the other aspects of Heidegger's thinking such as authenticity and so on?

Graham Harman: My major objection to Heidegger's standpoint is his *Dasein*-centrism. This proves his deep indebtedness to Kant, since even if you think Kant believes very strongly in the things-in-themselves, all that matters for Kant is the human-world relation. He finds it impossible to say anything about the collision of two billiard balls or the event of cotton burning fire, unless there is a human witness on the scene. Kant is perhaps the third greatest philosopher of all time (trailing only Plato/Aristotle or Aristotle/Plato, depending on my mood), but his influence has had at least this one very damaging effect. Everything always comes back to the interplay of human and world; the human is always one ingredient in every situation that can be discussed. This is not even a clearly formed doctrine in contemporary philosophy, but an atmospheric assumption.

In order to counter the *Dasein*-centric aspects of Heidegger, I focused heavily on a speculative metaphysical reading of the tool-analysis, and downplayed the existential analytic of *Dasein* in my interpretation. And I think it was crucially important to do so. But if there is one way in which my reading of Heidegger has changed over the past decade, it's that I have come to appreciate him again as an analyst of the human condition. On both of my last two readings of *Being and Time*, I was surprised to be so impressed by the analytic of everydayness and also by Heidegger's remarks about history, which seemed more insightful than I recalled.

Paul John Ennis: It is clear that you take an interest in neglected thinkers such as Gaston Bachelard or Bruno Latour. Can you tell us which thinkers have had the strongest impact on your thinking and why? Further, by rediscovering neglected thinkers such as Xavier

Zubiri do you think that object-oriented philosophy is reviving a forgotten tradition that we managed to lose sight of? If not can you tell us about any isolated predecessors with whom you feel an affinity?

Graham Harman: The obvious thinkers who have had a great impact on me are Heidegger, Husserl, Whitehead, Zubiri, and Latour. But let me name a few others in chronological order. First, José Ortega y Gasset. I was reading Ortega before I was reading Heidegger. He writes brilliantly (he nearly won the Nobel Prize for Literature), and is probably one of the two major influences on my writing style. I've tried to emulate his clarity as well as the light touch with which he incorporates erudition in his works. I also love Ortega's commitment to writing newspaper articles and other non-standard genres of philosophy rather than dull, plodding treatises. I've heard him referred to as "the intelligible Heidegger," so in some ways he may have paved the way for my acceptance of Heidegger a bit later. Finally, if there is one essay by anyone that prefigures all of my philosophical ideas, it is surely Ortega's "Essay in Esthetics by Way of a Preface," found in English in *Phenomenology and Art*. I discuss that essay in detail in *Guerrilla Metaphysics*. It's a startling masterpiece, though Ortega himself went no further along that trail.

Second, I should mention my original mentor Alphonso Lingis, the most dazzling prose stylist and most interesting human character I've ever known. He's one of the few people who took phenomenology in any sort of realist direction. In American Continental philosophy he is left somewhat at the fringes. That is to say, he's sort of an amusing character people tell nice jokes and stories about, and is respected to some extent, but is nowhere near the center of philosophical debate. And I consider this to be something of an indictment of the scene in America: when all is said and done, Lingis was one of the few original thinkers to be found in American Continental philosophy between 1970-2000. A lot of important translation and commentary was done during that period, but few people were in the same league as Lingis in terms of original ideas, and of course no one remotely equaled him as a writer. If Ortega's clarity and liveliness was the first thing I tried to emulate as a writer, Lingis's exoticism and spookiness was the second.

Third, Emmanuel Levinas. The fact that Lingis had translated so much Levinas made me wonder what the appeal was. And *Existence and Existents* had an immediate impact on me. No one – I repeat, no one – is a better reader of Heidegger than Levinas. He takes Heidegger so seriously, but without ever lapsing into a pious attitude toward him. It was Levinas who first showed me how to be a Heideggerian and an innovator at the same time, even though I think Levinas takes the wrong fork in the road.

Paul John Ennis: I've often felt that object-oriented philosophy was missing a trick when they overlook the "pre-transcendental idealist phenomenology" of Edmund Husserl. Would it be possible to read your breakthrough from Heidegger as a return to the earliest phenomenological analyses of Husserl?

Graham Harman: Yes! Husserl is badly out of fashion these days, and it often feels that I'm fighting a losing battle in my circles of friends when insisting on his importance. Last summer (2008) I went back and reread the whole of the *Logical Investigations*, and it was a pleasure despite the work's obvious difficulty.

The empiricist doctrine that things of the senses are nothing but bundles of qualities enjoys widespread acceptance even among those who otherwise denounce empiricism. The real greatness of Husserl is to have challenged, and in my view destroyed, the notion of a bundle of qualities. Everyone wants to reject Husserl for being an idealist, but many of these same people rush to embrace Badiou, who is no less an idealist than Husserl! While I obviously dislike Husserl's idealism, he is the first object-oriented idealist, followed in this respect by Merleau-Ponty and very few others. Even if we are trapped in a phenomenal realm, this realm displays a mighty duel between various trees or houses on one side and the wildly shifting profiles or adumbrations through which we grasp them on the other.

In my philosophy, this rift between intentional objects and their qualities is one of four great tensions that make up the fabric of the cosmos, all of them involving the polarization between an object-pole and a quality-pole. In my recent writings this has become a new fourfold of time, space, essence, and *eidos*. Without Husserl object-oriented philosophy could not exist, despite his idealism.

Paul John Ennis: Finally, as somebody who has been through it all before what advice do you have for somebody just starting off with Heidegger?

Graham Harman: *History of the Concept of Time* (not to be confused with the very brief *The Concept of Time*) is a good first thing to read. It contains most of the best content of *Being and Time*, along with the brilliant 100-page opening about Husserl and his greatest contributions to philosophy. It's also much better written than *Being and Time*, since it was a lecture course for undergraduates. Although almost everything by Heidegger is being translated into English now, there is no substitute for reading him in the original. As for advice on how to learn enough German to do so, my method was simply to plug away seriously for ten years looking up all the words that I didn't know. I also benefited greatly from summer language courses in Germany, one in Bremen and the other in Leipzig. There are plenty of summer courses available, and grants can often be had to attend them.

For American students of Continental philosophy in particular, it's also important not to become too sucked into Europhilia. The world is a lot bigger than France and Germany, rich though their intellectual traditions are. It's a good idea to put one foot in any non-Western tradition, just to make your mental world larger. And moreover, I would encourage American students to discover the American intellectual tradition as well, which is something we tend not to do. In philosophy there's William James, who may not be of the magnitude of Heidegger, but he can still teach you a lot about how to think and write. In literature and history there are all kinds of important people; Poe happens to be my favorite, just as he was the favorite of the French. In political philosophy, the United States has an impressive list of figures. If you're Canadian, don't you realize how important Marshall McLuhan really is? He's really big. In fact, people have no idea how big he is. We've only barely begun to appreciate McLuhan.

My point is that young North Americans, especially in the United States, who work in Continental philosophy, have a tendency to feel insecure in relation to Europe, the motherland of most of what we read in our discipline. It is vital to overcome this insecurity if you ever want to do more than write book reports about famous Europeans. Becoming familiar with the best home grown intellectual work is one excellent way to do that. Whenever I enter a bookstore in the States, my first trip is to the Library of America rack. Don't be like T.S. Eliot and think that we're from a half-savage country with nothing to contribute in intellectual matters. That's not how they think in Analytic philosophy or the hard sciences, let alone on Wall Street.

Paul John Ennis: If you had the chance to give your younger self advice on graduate school, what would it be?

Graham Harman: Finish it off. Graduate school is a finite training period, not a crucial battleground for the soul. Do your student assignments quickly and competently. It's fairly unlikely that you will be doing your mature philosophical work before your mid-thirties, so there is little point in the sort of procrastinating anguish in which I and others indulged. Don't indulge in psychological melodrama about conflicts with professors. You may have to swallow a few unpleasant incidents, because professors aren't always nice to students. But that doesn't mean they don't want you to finish. Take them for what they are, and move on. I should also speak a bit about the dissertation stage, which is where many students fall dead to the ground. Here, I think most destruction is self-destruction. The two main causes of self-destruction by graduate students are (1) perfectionism and (2) paranoia.

Let's start with perfectionism. It is often nothing more than a fear of being judged. This is an understandable fear, especially in the young who still have no track record of successes and are so much in need of positive feedback from their elders. As long as you are still working to perfect a piece of writing, you have a built-in shield against any criticism of it. "It's not done yet!" I also think there's an ingrained tendency among intelligent humans to defer and delay everything out of fear of success no less than fear of failure. Isn't it a frightening prospect that you might actually get the things you want? And so, quite often, we do a lot of work to make the objects of our desire seem inaccessible and far off in the distance. Many of the greatest moments in life, the moments where we finally get something really incredible that we had wanted for so long, are psychologically destabilizing moments. Part of us wants to avoid these rewards for various reasons. These are the tendencies you have to fight against if you want to finish your dissertation. I can assure you that life does look a lot better after you finish.

As for the "paranoia" part, in some ways it really is quite horrible to be a graduate student. There can be problems with one's professors and one's fellow students. At that stage you still feel too dependent on the favor of your professors. But don't feel that way, because they're always partly wrong about you. They have only the most superficial impressions of you. As a professor I constantly misjudge my students and which of them are the most serious, because I simply don't know them as well as their peers do. Students almost always rank each other more accurately than we rank them, because as a group we are suckers for attentive and charming students whose papers tell us the things we want to hear, and we tend to underrate the prickly rebels who are profiting from our lessons but not yet expressing it very well.

So try not to worry too much about what anyone says about your work at that stage. And don't worry if other students seem to be having more success than you are. Often enough, the teacher's pets and super achievers of their twenties burn out, while the ones who are struggling to articulate their ideas are the ones with the really important ideas. Personally, I tend to give everyone a free pass until some time in their thirties, because before that there's a sense in which we are merely seeing rehearsals of what a person might someday be.

On the subject of professors...there tends to be a handful of mean, nasty professors in any Department. But it is rarely a secret which ones they are. Graduate students gossip like crazy about their professors, and the older ones can tell you as soon as you arrive who the rotten ones are who will ruin your morale and maybe your life. So, just listen to those older students. If a professor has done terrible things to other students over the course of many years, what makes you think your case will be different? Simply avoid the harmful people on your faculty and spend time with the good ones.

Who was it who wrote that we all basically know which people and situations to avoid, but that "an imprudent curiosity" leads us to seek them out anyway? Don't have imprudent curiosity. It's simple. Don't choose an advisor because you think he or she is going to help you on the job market. I wouldn't even choose an advisor based entirely on dissertation topic. Choose a person you like and respect as a human character—one that is psychologically clean and won't mess with your mind. And if you do have problems with your advisor, then just change advisors! These things happen, and your Department does want you to finish; it makes them look better if you do. Don't wallow in whatever melodramatic problems you might be having with faculty members. This simply becomes another alibi not to get work done.

Paul John Ennis: What, in your opinion, is the future of post-Continental philosophy?

Graham Harman: First, I should say that I am no longer a believer in "bridging the gap" between Analytic and Continental philosophy, although there seems to be near-universal agreement that this is the task of the coming generation. In practice, this bridging of gaps seems to be an assimilationist project serving the interests of the Analytic establishment. What it really means is that the standard Continental heroes (Hegel, Heidegger) are restated in "mainstream" Analytic language, and I don't think the results are always fortunate. I would agree that Continental philosophers should read more Analytic thinkers, because there is much to learn from their style and their discoveries, but why go to extremes and say that the gap must be bridged? I'm a believer in one reality, not in one truth. The world contains many animal species and many religions, so why should there be only one school of philosophy? There should be a diverse ecosystem of thoughts. Unification movements always serve the interest of the dominant power of the moment, and in our case that happens to be Analytic philosophy. We should keep our minority movement going, we just need to purge it of some of its excesses. Over the past century Continental philosophy has been dogmatically anti-realist, and we've also spent far too much time commenting on past philosophers and believing that this is an automatically philosophical act. It can be, but often it is not. In recent decades, we've also relied too heavily on France to produce all the innovations for us. It's time to take responsibility for our own thinking.

As for where Continental philosophy will go next, allow me to develop the fantasy published some time ago on my blog. It is well known that I was one of the four original "speculative realist" philosophers, along with Ray Brassier, Iain Hamilton Grant, and Quentin Meillassoux. Despite the shared group name, there are only loose intellectual affinities among us. We're all realists, insofar as we all reject the Kantian impasse in philosophy. And we're all speculative, insofar as we do not defend a dull form of commonsense realism, but end up with some very strange conclusions.

The fantasy sketched on my blog was that perhaps the future of Continental philosophy will be nothing but a vast civil war between the four separate strands of speculative realism. This is not because we are important people, but because I think the four positions in question do give a fairly good selection of the possible new positions in Continental thought. Perhaps Grant is the "cyber-vitalist" who hints at new directions for the Deleuzian tradition. Brassier is the hardnosed, nihilistic science-lover who thinks that cognitive science will eliminate the "folk psychology" that he finds in phenomenology. Meillassoux, alone among the four of us, believes that the human-world correlate is inescapable and must be radicalized from within rather than assaulted from the outside. And my position is object-oriented metaphysics, which borrows from phenomenology on one side and Whitehead and Latour on the other. And I'm going to stick with this fantasy, and predict that the Continental philosophy of 2050 will be visibly descended from one or more of these branches.

Interview with Jeffrey Malpas

Paul John Ennis: It now seems likely that your book Heidegger's Topology: Being, Place, World *will remain the definitive work on topological issues in Heidegger for the foreseeable future. What lead you to write a book on an area previously considered peripheral by other Heidegger scholars?*

Jeffrey Malpas: I should say, first of all, that it hasn't been considered peripheral by all other Heidegger scholars. While Joe Fell's 1979 book, *Heidegger and Sartre: An Essay on Being and Place,* doesn't have the same aim as *Heidegger's Topology,* it does treat place as a key concept in Heidegger's thinking. Joe's book was an important touchstone for me when I was writing *Heidegger's Topology.* More directly to your question, I would say that the obvious reason for writing a book on topology in Heidegger and I should say, by way of clarification, that I refer to topography in relation to my own work, but use topology with more specific reference to Heidegger, is that, although many other scholars may have thought place to be peripheral in Heidegger's thinking, Heidegger did not. Not only does Heidegger take up and deploy topological ideas and images throughout his work, but it is Heidegger himself who characterizes his thinking as a "topology of being". The fact that the centrality of place in Heidegger's thinking has been generally overlooked is partly a result of the concentration of attention on *Being and Time* – a work in which both place and space figure in a highly problematic fashion. If one begins with the later writings, then the topological elements in Heidegger's thinking are impossible to avoid, and *Being and Time* itself appears in a different light. Moreover, it is not just that place is important to the reading of Heidegger's own work, but that Heidegger is a critical figure in the philosophical engagement with place. Essays such as "Building Dwelling Thinking" and "Art and Space" explicitly address issues of place in a way that is not matched by any previous thinker with the possible exception of Kant. Consequently, if one wishes to address the question of place philosophically, one has no choice but to take up Heidegger's own topological mode of thought.

Paul John Ennis: I've noticed that in Place and Experience: A Philosophical Topography *you mention important influences such as Edward Casey. Can you tell us a little bit about other formative influences on your intellectual development? Further can you tell us what attracted you to the relatively underdeveloped field of "philosophical topography"?*

Jeffrey Malpas: I think it was David Wood who suggested I look at Ed's work when I gave a paper that was the beginning of *Place and Experience* ("A Taste of Madeleine: Notes towards a Philosophy of Place") at the University of Warwick around 1992. Ed's work was very important in giving me the sense that I wasn't alone in what I wanted to do, and, along with a number of other close colleagues from geography and other disciplines as well as philosophy, he has been a constant source of support and stimulation ever since. Prior to *Place and Experience*, however, I was already developing a set of topographic ideas through notions of horizontality and locality. I made use of both these ideas in my first book, *Donald Davidson and the Mirror of Meaning*, which was itself a development out of my graduate work, while some of the connections between place, limit, and unity that have also been important in my recent work were present in my writing as an undergraduate – mainly through work on Kant and Aristotle. But my interest in place and topography also goes back much further than this. I grew up in New Zealand, a place in which there is always a strong sense of the natural environment.

My family also travelled a lot. My father and grandfather sold gadgets and toys at exhibitions, country shows, markets and suchlike – they were "grafters" according to the Northern English term my grandfather used, and by the time I was 13 we had been back and forth between the UK, Australia and New Zealand a number of times. I am sure that the New Zealand environment and the experience of travel between places contributed significantly to my topographical interests. At school I focused on History and English, writing on Herman Hesse, Friedrich Nietzsche and William Blake for my University scholarship exam - although none of these figures were actually taught in the formal curriculum. My undergraduate studies at the University of Auckland were in both Philosophy and History. I take History as itself connecting to place, not only because I view place as encompassing the temporal as well as the spatial, but also through the concept of memory as well as of site. I also read a great deal of literature – especially poetry. *Place and Experience* more or less begins with Wordsworth and Heaney, and in many ways that book is an attempt to articulate the sense of place that has usually only been addressed in art and literature. New Zealand writers were also important in my thinking at the time (and still are) – writers such as Witi Ihimaera (whom I have since been lucky enough to get to know), and poets from James K. Baxter to Sam Hunt. At Auckland I had some very influential teachers. One was Clive Pearson, an inspiring and provocative figure who introduced me to Heidegger; another was Krister Segerberg, who insisted I go on to graduate work in philosophy when I was not at all inclined to do so, and although a logician, also supported my developing interest in hermeneutics; yet another was Martin Tweedale, who schooled me in Aristotle and Aquinas; and a fourth was Julian Young, with whom I have maintained a long and close association.

One of the things that characterized my undergraduate training, and for which I am very grateful, was the fact that it was strongly focused on the history of philosophy including the history of the Analytic tradition, and on the reading of primary texts – something much less common in philosophy departments nowadays. In addition, I was very lucky to be part of a small group of fellow students with similar or overlapping interests, including, most notably, Carl Page - a philosopher who is now at St John's in Annapolis. I was an undergraduate, and then a Masters student, at Auckland during the late Seventies and early Eighties, and that time also had its impact. 1977 was my first year at University, and it coincided with the appearance of punk as well as the rise of ska and reggae, which should be viewed, I think, as the late Seventies analogue to the protest and alternative movements of the Sixties. In both cases political concerns merged with musical and artistic forms – albeit very different ones. For all that punk may have been viewed as musically and artistically crude, it also had roots in a strong political and cultural sensibility that actually thematized issues of commitment and community, participation and action, belonging and alienation, and even place and identity. Music, including jazz, blues, rock and folk, as well as classical continues to be important to me – and also connects up, often quite directly, with my interest in place, not only through the influence and expression of place in music (consider, in classical music, some of Vaughan Williams' work), but also through the way sound provides an often over-looked aspect of our engagement with place (here the work of experimental sound artists from John Cage to Brian Eno is especially relevant).

From Auckland, I went on to do graduate work at the ANU (Australian National University) in Canberra, where Phillip Pettit and Jack Smart were my main advisors. Also at the ANU, as a Research Fellow, was Fred D'Agostino with whom I later worked in my first academic job at the University of New England. He was extremely supportive, and my early ideas were very much developed in conversation with Fred's work, which is largely at the intersection of political philosophy and philosophy of science, and overlaps in interesting ways with my own. Richard Rorty was also at the ANU during part of my time there, and his work was extremely important, not because it had any direct relevance to place, but because of the way he combined Analytic and Continental thinking. At that stage I was already trying to read Gadamer and Heidegger alongside Davidson as well as von Wright, Collingwood and Wittgenstein, but Rorty gave that reading a new sense and direction. Aside from Heidegger, to whom I stand, in any case, in a somewhat different relation, it is Davidson and Gadamer who are probably the two most important philosophical influences on my work, and I feel very privileged to have known both of them – Gadamer, while I was a Humboldt fellow in Heidelberg towards the end of his long life, and Davidson, from the early 1990s onwards which is when I first visited Berkeley, and also, of course, when I first got to know Bert Dreyfus.

There are two other names that I should mention as having a significant impact on my thinking, although only through their writing: one is Albert Camus, and the other is Hannah Arendt. Arendt is someone I have come to fairly late, but her work has become more important as I have engaged more directly with issues of politics and the public realm. Camus has always been a favorite of mine, and not because of any existentialist connection. I am not especially sympathetic to existentialism even though I have written on it, have often taught it, and would probably be viewed as drawing on existentialist ideas, and that partly reflects my discomfort with Sartre, as well as a more general concern with what I take to be subjectivist and voluntarist elements in certain existentialist thinking. Camus is, for me, a lyrical thinker, whose politics connects up with much of what I find valuable in Arendt, and whose sense of place, as well as of human finitude as that is worked out in place, comes across very clearly in his writing, especially his essays. Just as music and poetry have had an important influence on my thinking, so too do I find the visual arts to be significant also. From a New Zealand perspective, the painter Colin McCahon presents an especially salient example of an artist for whom issues of place and identity loom large, and for whom those issues are also connected to ideas concerning language and the sign, the latter understood both in their meaning and materiality, as well as of the spirit. You will notice that McCahon works appear on the covers of both *Place and Experience* and *Heidegger's Topology*, and I hope also to use two other McCahon works for the monographs on which I am now working: *Ethos and Topos* and *Triangulating Davidson*. Among other artists who I find of particular interest are Turner (not least because of the obviously topographic nature of much of his work), Cezanne (an obvious point of connection for a Heideggerian), Anselm Kiefer, Gerhard Richter, and Joseph Beuys, Robert Morris (partly because of his own work with Davidson, but for much more besides), the 19th century Tasmanian landscape artist John Glover, contemporary Aboriginal painters such as Kathleen Petyarre, land artists such as Andy Goldsworthy although this is something that Ed Casey has been exploring much more than I have, and also digital artists such as Char Davies (whose work I have only recently discovered).

The engagement with creative artists has, in fact, become quite an important part of my own work. I have supervised students in the area, and have also been closely involved with a number of exhibitions; writing catalogues essays and being involved with aspects of curation. This engagement has itself had a significant impact on my thinking, partly through the way in which it has required me to consider how one can and should engage philosophically with artworks, but also through drawing attention to the interplay between work and place in both its temporal and spatial aspects.

Paul John Ennis: You've made inroads into the ethical demands of a philosophical topography i.e. the link between ethos and topos. Did you find it particularly difficult to address the questions of place and ethics in Heidegger or did you find, as many deep ecologists have, that the ideas outstrip the thinker at the level of ethics?

Jeffrey Malpas: One of the main projects I am currently working on is a book on just this topic – the ethics and politics of place. One reason for doing so is that there is a widespread view, one that probably has its classic philosophical statement in Levinas' work, that place is inevitably connected with exclusion and violence, and with reactionary and conservative forms of politics. Heidegger is often taken to exemplify just this connection. That there is a different potential in Heidegger's work, however, seems to me to be demonstrated by the way aspects of Heidegger's philosophy are developed and deployed in thinkers such as Arendt and Gadamer. But I also think that paying closer attention to the topographical elements of Heidegger's thought itself shows a very different political and ethical potential from that which is usually assumed. Far from being exclusionary, I would argue that place both gathers and enables engagement at the same time as it opens up plurality and difference. It is place that allows the encounter with the other, at the same time as it allows the demand of the other to be made real. Of course, ideas always outstrip the thinker in the sense that those ideas that have real significance always retain a richness that goes beyond the particular way in which they are taken up on any specific occasion – this is partly what I refer to in *Heidegger's Topology* as the iridescence that attaches to key philosophical terms and concepts – and I see no reason to suppose that Heidegger should be an exception here, although neither do I think this makes his work especially problematic in this regard.

Paul John Ennis: You've published a lot of articles, edited a whole bunch of collections, and written a few books. How do you manage to remain so prolific and can you give us a little bit of advice about writing good philosophy today? You've also got a number of papers available online. Do you think the internet is drastically changing the academic world? Have you had any thoughts on the peculiar public space that the internet has come to occupy in our collective minds?

Jeffrey Malpas: I don't regard myself as very prolific – in fact, I constantly feel that there is too much that I have not yet written or properly worked out. I do think that there is a discipline to writing. Writing is a task, a piece of work, to which one has to set oneself. Too often, we seem to expect writing to come easily, but, at least when it is philosophical writing that is at issue, it is very seldom that it happens that way. If I do have a reasonably steady rate of production, that is partly because I often find it hard to turn down invitations – and a lot of my writing now is a response to requests to produce pieces for specific occasions or publications. I keep resolving to say "no" more often, but it doesn't always happen. As a result, however, I am probably often pressed to produce work more quickly than I would like, although I have almost come to accept the fact that this may be unavoidable. I am a bit wary of offering advice of how to write "good" philosophy. What I would say, however, is that I do think the best philosophical writing comes out of a real sense of engagement with the subject matter that also attends closely to the concepts and texts at issue, and through having a passion and commitment to understand (and most often genuine understanding comes through doing the actual work of writing) and to communicate that understanding. Unfortunately, there is a lot of published work that doesn't engage in this fashion, which simply works the machinery, as it were, or else just remains at too superficial or simplistic a level.

There is no doubt that the internet is having an impact on academia, although the exact nature of that impact, beyond the most immediate effects, is not easy to discern. Certainly it has changed, among other things, the way we communicate, the way we gain access to journals, and the way we undertake research. I am very cautious, however, about claims regarding the supposedly radical impact of new technology. We have a tendency to misidentify the exact nature of that impact and often, I think, to exaggerate it. The claims of many so-called "trans-humanists", for instance, seem to me to exhibit a failure to attend to the nature and limits of the technologies at issue as well as to the character of human existence. Arendt says in *The Human Condition* that "it is still probable that the enormous changes of the industrial revolution behind us and the even greater changes of the atomic revolution before us will remain changes of the world and not changes in the basic condition of human life on earth". Like Arendt, I do not think that the changes wrought by technology, represent changes in the basic ontological condition of human life, although they certainly result in major changes in the way those conditions are realized. The internet, and associated issues regarding information and communication technologies more generally, is something I have written about in a few places (for instance, in the essay I published in 2000 titled "Acting at a Distance And Knowing from Afar: Agency and Knowledge on the World Wide Web", and also in some of my recent work on cultural heritage). Given the possible implications of new technologies for thinking about place, this is an area of inquiry into which I am constantly being drawn.

One final comment: so far as contemporary changes in the academic world are concerned, it seems to me that the changes being wrought, at least in Australasia, the United Kingdom, and in much of Europe, are probably less directly to do with the internet as with the subordination of the academy to the interests and directions of government. Previously this was something we were only familiar with from the centrally-planned regimes of the communist world. But now thinking (along with teaching) has itself become an industry, regulated, not by the requirements of thinking as such, but by contemporary audit and assurance practice, and according to national research priorities and party political interest. The effect this is having on contemporary academic work is pretty disastrous, and it is amazing that, as academics, we have generally been fairly passive in the face of these changes. Indeed, in many ways, we have ourselves assisted in the undermining of the qualities and structures including the values and modes of conduct that have shaped the academic professions, that have formed us as researchers, thinkers and teachers, and that have been essential in enabling and fostering to the pursuit of knowledge especially qualities such as dissent, diversity, independence, and self-directness. For many of us who are committed to what Arendt calls "the life of the mind", this is an enormously dangerous and depressing development.

Paul John Ennis: Your philosophical topography manages to take the best from both the Analytic and Continental traditions. Do you think we tend to overplay the division to the detriment of philosophy outside of the academy?

Jeffrey Malpas: I am not sure if the division is very much noticed outside of the academy, and it certainly doesn't seem to figure very much (if at all) in the popular philosophy books that abound nowadays. Is the distinction overplayed? I am not sure that it is, and in fact, it seems to me that the tendency to downplay the division that also crops up increasingly now is often associated with the privileging of Analytic philosophy – thus good Continental philosophy comes to be the Continental philosophy that is done by Analytic philosophers. In fact, whatever the real philosophical differences that underpin the division, the most salient fact about it is probably the way in which it works out or is expressed politically. The division between Analytic and Continental often has a very real and direct impact in terms of hiring, tenure, and promotion decisions, in funding allocations, in the ranking of departments and schools, and in Faculty, University and sometimes Government policy frameworks. I think this is extremely unfortunate, especially given the vigor with which so many of our colleagues seem to pursue the goal of what often seems to be little more than a form of philosophical Puritanism. Moreover, from my own experience on grants bodies and elsewhere, the antagonism that exists between different modes of philosophizing, while not often noticed outside the Academy, is frequently a source of significant damage to the discipline from within. Philosophers are thus sometimes seen as incapable of getting their own house in order, and as more concerned to preserve their own sense of the rigor of the discipline (no matter how partial that may be), than to protect and further the interests of the discipline as a whole. I think this is a most distressing situation, and one that doesn't show any obvious signs of changing in spite of the rhetoric of inclusion and diversity that occasionally rises to prominence.

Paul John Ennis: You have three works forthcoming, but I'd like to focus on The Place of Landscape: Concepts, Contexts, Studies. *What can we expect from this work and does it represent a kind of culmination of a "topological turn" in contemporary philosophy i.e. that as an edited collection there are now enough topological thinkers to warrant such a project?*

Jeffrey Malpas: I have had a longstanding interest in the issue of landscape and was especially taken by Ed Casey's 2002 book on the subject, *Representing Place*. I certainly wouldn't say that *The Place of Landscape* is the culmination of a topological turn, but it might constitute one expression of that turn. There can be no doubt that there are now a number of thinkers across a range of disciplines who are taking up the notion of place in various ways. Not just Ed Casey or myself, nor even pioneers such as Edward Relph and David Seaman, but many others (some of whom have themselves been working in the area for a very long time) including, to cite just a few examples, scholars like Nick Entrikin, Philip Sheldrake, Keith Basso, Stuart Elden, Anna Godlewska, David Morris, and Deborah Bird Rose. Unfortunately, not too many of them are in philosophy – or at least, not in mainstream English-speaking philosophy, where place, if it is addressed at all, is too often treated as an almost entirely secondary phenomenon of little or no interest in its own right. The aim of *The Place of Landscape* is to address the connection between place and landscape. It brings together a number of writers from quite different disciplinary backgrounds (the range of disciplines represented includes philosophy, geography, art history and theory, environmentalism, anthropology, film theory, garden history, landscape studies, literature, and theology) in order to explore the idea of landscape in its positive as well as its more negative aspects, and to set out a way of viewing landscape as itself one of the ways in which place is formed, and also, therefore, one of the modes of our own self-formation.

The other two edited works that I have currently in press – *Consequences of Hermeneutics* (with Santiago Zabala) and *Dialogues with Davidson* – are not topographical in their primary orientation, as your own focus on *The Place of Landscape* might indicate, but they do represent two important areas that, at least as I see matters, connect closely with matters of place and topography. Hermeneutics is itself essentially attuned to a topographical perspective and mode of approach (something evident in both Heidegger and Gadamer's emphasis on hermeneutic situatedness), while I view Davidson as, like Heidegger, a thinker whose work should also be understood as constituting a form of topology or topography in its own right (a reading that I have of course developed in books like *Donald Davidson and the Mirror of Meaning*, as well as in a number of subsequent essays – it is also one of the themes of *Triangulating Davidson*). I might mention two other directions in which my work is also moving. One is the engagement with ethics that I briefly discussed earlier, which not only takes issue with certain ethical critiques of place-oriented thinking, but which also looks to understand ethics in a topographic fashion, and so also in terms of our concrete ethical engagement. The other focuses around something I am staring to refer to as "romantic materialism", and that is concerned to explore and articulate the conjunction between certain themes evident in romanticism (broadly construed) and the emphasis on the material placedness that is also part of topographic thinking, This conjunction is evident, in a particularly intriguing way, it seems to me, in the work of people like Peter Ackroyd and Ian Sinclair, as well as in the thinkers, writers and artists to whom their work is related (Machen, Blake, Nash and others), or that are part of the same contemporary constellation (Moorcock, for instance, or Patrick Keiller), although it also extends to a much wider body of material, including writers such as W. G. Sebald and also Walter Benjamin, Proust as well as Heidegger, and that is often more artistic and literary than explicitly philosophical (Benjamin is an especially interesting figure in this regard). This work is very much geared to issues concerning the connections between narrativity, memory and place, and the realization of memory and identity in concretized, material forms.

Although there are people working in cultural theory, cultural geography, and at the edges of philosophy on some of these themes – mostly around notions of collective memory, nostalgia and loss, objects and identity – much of this work tends to be weak in terms of its conceptual articulation or its philosophical or theoretical foundation (sometimes explicitly eschewing such foundations), or else assumes (often in ill-defined ways) a constructionist or even subjectivist perspective. Part of what motivates me here is to find a way of integrating an otherwise disparate range of materials concerning issues of landscape, the materialized forms of memory, the role of story (often understood in terms of movement and journey) in the formation of self, the interconnection of the poetic and the placed, the role of the image and the working of art, the embeddedness of mythic, religious and imaginative forms in sites and pathways (both urban and non-urban, in the indigenous thinking of country, and in European folk traditions and stories, and even in fairy-tales – Marina Warner's work comes to mind here). My aim, in short, is to explore the interplay between the "romantic" (in the sense that this might be applied even to Benjamin's work) and the "material" (where this refers us to an emphasis on the concrete actuality of the things around us, and to our own embodied, situated mode of existence). Place, of course, is the term that draws this together, since, on my account, place is the materialization of the romantic and the romanticized form of the material.

Paul John Ennis: If you had the chance to give your younger self advice on graduate school what would it be?

Jeffrey Malpas: I should say that I am in two minds about the question you have asked me here: on the one hand I recognize how much careers are influenced by place of study and the people with whom one studies; on the other I am uncomfortable with the careerist tendencies that seem to have become so dominant in parts of the discipline. I am also very dubious of the current obsession with ranking. I guess I still harbor the perhaps naïve idea that merit ought to be recognized no matter from where it comes. My own case is probably somewhat idiosyncratic. When I completed my Masters in 1981, I applied for a scholarship that would ordinarily have taken me to Oxford or Cambridge (then the usual destination for New Zealanders studying overseas). But the UK Government had just imposed fees on Commonwealth students and the New Zealand Grants Committee had also removed overseas tenure on its own scholarships. So although I had a scholarship from the New Zealand

Government, I couldn't use it as people had in the past. At the same time we also had our first child on the way, and so while I considered North America, it looked too difficult in the circumstances. In the end applied for, and was offered, a scholarship at the ANU in Canberra, and went there at the end of 1982. Would anything I know now have changed what I did then? I suspect not, because my choices were so much constrained by circumstance. I do think, however, that it would probably have made a very big difference to my career if it had been a year or so earlier when I completed, and I had therefore been able, as was more usual at the time, to go on to Oxford or Cambridge – although one consequence may well have been that my career, and perhaps my thinking, would have taken a more orthodox course! For New Zealand and Australian students now, the question is whether to try for a place in the US or the UK, or whether to stay in Australasia. This is not an easy choice, and it probably depends too much on individual circumstance to be able to give any across-the-board advice. What I would say, however, is that finding a supervisor with whom you can work well and a place that fits your interests is probably the most important consideration, and after that the issue of the supposed reputation of the department or school.

Paul John Ennis: What, in your opinion, is the future of post-Continental philosophy?

Jeffrey Malpas: The language of "post-Continental" seems to echo the language of "post-Analytic" that was so common twenty years ago, and I actually don't think a lot has changed over that period. There are more people doing work that crosses traditions now, but anything that might correspond to the "post-Continental" seems to me, at present, to be scattered and somewhat dispersed, while the lines between the Analytic and the Continental remain still pretty solid – it is just the way those lines are expressed that has shifted somewhat. I don't think we can say how philosophy will develop in the future, although I do think what has been happening is that Analytic philosophy has, if anything, become rather narrower than in the past, and, at least in Australasia, is generally not faring well institutionally (although there are some exceptions). Much as I would like to see a more open, engaged, and vibrant form of philosophy developing that is not bound by ideology, such a hope seems overly optimistic, and it is certainly not helped by current developments in higher education in the UK or Australasia.

Interview with Stuart Elden

Paul John Ennis: You navigate an unusual academic path that traverses disciplines such as geography, politics, and philosophy. In many ways they seem to complement each other quite well. Why do you think it has taken so long for philosophy to expand into areas such as geography once again? Further, what do you think philosophy has to learn from your own discipline of geography?

Stuart Elden: My first degree was in Politics and Modern History, and in studying that I became interested in political theory. I had two remarkable teachers of theory in my final year as an undergraduate – Barbara Goodwin and Mark Neocleous – and they were an inspiration. They both made me feel that I could follow ideas where they led, which would often take me to other disciplines or other parts of the library. My final year dissertation led to an offer of a PhD place, and I began work with Barbara and David Wootton, who was a historian of ideas. David taught me a great deal about how to approach texts, how to read them in contexts and made it very clear I had a long way to go. After about a year, because of the direction my research was taking, I transferred to Mark as supervisor, which continued until I completed. Mark was excellent in toughening me up by challenging most of what I wrote, and giving me other things to read. So my advisors were pushing me in different directions, outside of the politics background I had, and into reading philosophy and work in the history of ideas.

The interest in geography came about because I was interested in questions of spatiality – and, particularly in the PhD thesis, the relation of spatiality to history. This meant I began reading some of the geographers who had engaged with theory, particularly Heidegger, Foucault and Lefebvre who I was reading at the time. This led me to read people like David Harvey, Nigel Thrift, Ed Soja and Derek Gregory. While still in a politics department – my first job post-PhD was teaching politics at Warwick University – I started publishing in geography journals like *Antipode* and *Political Geography*. When *Mapping the Present* (the book based on the thesis) came out, it was being reviewed and discussed by geographers more than other disciplines. So in that sense a move into a geography department, in retrospect, feels natural. At the time I wasn't at all sure, but the department seemed willing to take a risk with me. Durham Geography has been an intellectually very stimulating place to be, where I feel able to work on politics and theory as much as more traditionally "geographical" topics.

My current work – which has actually been "the next book" for almost a decade – is an attempt to write a history of the concept of territory, a kind of genealogy that tries to trace the pre-history of the term well before it took on its modern sense. It's a very political book; it reads philosophers from Plato and Aristotle on; and is concerned with an obviously geographical theme. So yes, I'd certainly agree that these interests complement each other well. And yes, philosophers traditionally did work on all these issues. In the "Continental" tradition, I'm not sure that has ever really changed. There is a strong spatial sense in Nietzsche, for instance, as well as the twentieth century thinkers that I've worked on or who are popular in geography today. Husserl lectured on space; Merleau-Ponty provided some intriguing analyses, especially around the body; Deleuze and Guattari of course, Derrida etc. And political philosophy, or at least philosophers talking about politics, has continued. Marxism, for instance, and there have been some very interesting Marxist philosophers with an interest in space. So it's perhaps only certain ways of thinking about philosophy that has neglected questions of spatiality.

In geography as a discipline there has been a real interest in contemporary philosophy or social theory more generally for several years, developing in all sorts of interesting ways. Political geography as a subfield has perhaps been a bit slower in doing this than cultural or urban geography, for instance, but it happens across human geography. For a while in the 1970s and early 1980s Marxism was the key element, and while to an extent that continues, a whole range of other thinkers have been discussed and appropriated. Recently I've been interested in bringing out these engagements more explicitly—the *Foucault and Geography* book I co-edited with Jeremy Crampton or the *Reading Kant's Geography* book Eduardo Mendieta and I have coming out, which tries to create a conversation between geographers, philosophers and others around this neglected text. The work I've done on Henri Lefebvre has been at the intersection of these interests in politics, philosophy and geography.

Paul John Ennis: There has been some talk about a topological turn in philosophy incorporating a wide array of thinkers, but also giving rise to schools of thinking such as eco-phenomenology. What do you think of this trend and how do you see it playing out in the future?

Stuart Elden: Yes, there has been some remarkable work. Jeff Malpas and Ed Casey, for instance. Ed's *The Fate of Place* book was really important for me, and was an inspiration for what I hope to accomplish with the history of the concept of territory book. There are some disagreements, perhaps particularly around the term "topological", but I'd like to think some of my work has contributed to those debates. There have been some really interesting works in environmental philosophy that have drawn on Heidegger and other writers, and of an earlier generation people like David Seamon and Yi-Fu Tuan drew on phenomenology and other philosophical traditions in their geographical work. I'm not terribly familiar with some of this work but dialogue between geographers and philosophers would certainly be worthwhile. Recently I think Peter Sloterdijk's work is worthy of attention. There have been a couple of special issues on his work, and translations of recent texts are coming out. His three volume *Sphären, Spheres*, is supposed to be coming out too, which will be a real event. He says that one way to think of it is as the "Being and Space" to partner Heidegger's *Being and Time*. It's basically a book about being-with, about *Mitsein*.

Paul John Ennis: What is it about Martin Heidegger and Michel Foucault in particular that attracted your attention? As a non-philosopher by trade can you tell us a little bit about what it was like to first encounter Heidegger and the associated challenges such as the considerable scholarly output, his unique German, and so on?

Stuart Elden: I came to Heidegger through Foucault, though I have since made the claim that it makes sense of Foucault to see him through his engagement with Heidegger. Foucault was a terrific writer – *Discipline and Punish* obviously, but *The History of Madness* and *The Birth of the Clinic* too. More recently I've been writing pieces on the Foucault lectures as they come out, with a view to a book on them some day. There are some remarkable analyses in the lectures: I was particularly struck by the ones of the mid-1970s on Psychiatric Power and The Abnormals. Back then I became really interested in the genealogical approach, and wanted to do some work on how he developed this from Nietzsche. Then the spatial angle came in – how does Foucault make his histories spatial histories? – and I felt certain that the way he worked some of these things through couldn't be straight-forwardly traced through Nietzsche. I was intrigued by his comment about Heidegger being the "essential philosopher" and wanted to see what, if anything, there was to this.

In terms of the engagement with Heidegger – well it was hard work! Some time into my PhD I wished I had done an MA in Continental Philosophy, since this would undoubtedly have made things a little easier. I'd done one undergraduate course in philosophy, though Heidegger hadn't featured, but I at least had some sense of Kant, Hegel and Nietzsche. I'd also been taught and then, in the PhD, began teaching, the history of political thought. So I suppose I had some background. The first Heidegger book I read was *Being and Time,* in the Macquarrie and Robinson translation. This was a real challenge but I can't think of any other book I've read that has had such an impact on me. It raised so many questions and opened up areas that I wanted to work on. I spent the summer that year in France and took a box of Heidegger books with me, and worked through them while I was there. The Nietzsche lectures were really important to the project. While I was there I realized that there were important texts not available in English – the Hölderlin lectures especially – but some of these were available in French. So I read them in French, and used them to help me read the German. In time, I was able to muddle through the German. I can't really read German but I could read Heidegger in German. You learn the specialized vocabulary and his particular style is actually a benefit. It's hard to read Heidegger in English without picking up something of the German – one of the reasons I prefer the Macquarrie and Robinson translation to the Stambaugh one is that it makes it clear how difficult it is to render Heidegger into English, and how important it is to get the nuances of German words.

Another thing that's worth noting is that a lot of the areas of philosophy Heidegger wrote about were ones I had little or no knowledge of. So I'd try to read Aristotle before I read Heidegger on Aristotle, and so on. Obviously that can't completely fill in the gaps, but it gave me a bit of a sense of what was interesting or distinctive about what Heidegger was doing. It meant I read a lot of the tradition, but that I have some odd gaps – Spinoza, for instance – since Heidegger didn't really write on him. I've tried to fill in some of those absences since. Most recently, for the territory book, I've been reading medieval political theology extensively. Speaking of Spinoza it is interesting how much he is invoked today, when it is often Deleuze's Spinoza... I do put quite a lot of emphasis on the importance of reading the primary texts, and of at least carefully comparing the translations to the original language.

Paul John Ennis: Speaking Against Number *is a book that confidently encompasses the entire span of Heidegger's thinking. Did you feel, when you decided to tackle Heidegger that complacency had begun to set into the Heidegger scholarship? Where should the topologically inclined among us go to examine Heidegger on the question of topology?*

Stuart Elden: Well, this wasn't my first attempt to tackle Heidegger. More of *Mapping the Present* is on Heidegger than Foucault, and the Heidegger work had continued in some shorter pieces, especially on the *Beiträge*. I was interested in the question of calculation and didn't feel I'd done that justice in the previous book. There were some issues around politics I wanted to explore, and I had a couple of conference papers on Heidegger's early engagement with Aristotle on the *logos* and rhetoric. It took me a while to see how I could pull the concerns with language, politics and calculation together into a single coherent book, but that's what *Speaking Against Number* tries to do. The title is to be read as a phrase and as three separate ways of thinking politics — rhetorically, polemically and calculatively.

In doing the book I did read the whole *Gesamtausgabe*, as it existed then, in chronological order. That threw up a whole load of interesting themes. So, yes, instead of the 1950s work on technology I looked more at the 1930s work on machination, etc. I suppose it was an attempt to look at some less explored parts of his work. The 1920s Heidegger has been treated magnificently by people like Theodore Kisiel and John van Buren, but there is less good work on the 1930s, which is really a crucial decade for Heidegger in all sorts of reasons. I also focused less on texts I'd discussed in detail in *Mapping the Present* — the Nietzsche lectures, for instance. While I still get new volumes of the *Gesamtausgabe* as they come out, I've not read Heidegger since finishing that book and a couple of articles that were outtakes from that analysis. Maybe one day I will go back to him, but for now I feel I've said all I have to say about him.

Heidegger on spatiality and topology comes up in all sorts of places. The *What is a Thing?* and the Hölderlin lectures in the 1930s, later essays like "Building Dwelling Thinking", "The Thing", and "Art and Space" would be good places to start. Jeff Malpas's *Heidegger's Topology* would be an excellent place to go for a commentary, which would also lead you to the right primary texts.

Paul John Ennis: You make a number of bold claims in Speaking Against Number *such as the claim that* Being and Time *is not an apolitical work or that there is a "rhetorical excess" inscribed into the early work of Heidegger. In many ways this is a direct challenge to the idea that one can separate Heidegger's politics from his philosophy (especially for those who draw a line between* Being and Time *and the later work on this basis). What do you think the implications of this are for Heideggerians or do you think, as you seem to argue in the last part of the book, Heidegger finally comes to see National Socialism as nothing more than another manifestation of the Gestell? Do you think this is enough or do you find an ethical lack in this realization i.e. it ought to have been evident on a basis other than technology?*

Stuart Elden: Yes, I'd see it as a challenge in those terms. The real revelation for me was reading the early lecture courses, especially those on Aristotle. The Plato's *Sophist* course and the one that preceded it on the *Basic Concepts of Aristotelian Philosophy* are remarkable. In reading those it became clear that certain lines or passages of *Being and Time* rested on a much wider foundation that he'd developed in dialogue with Aristotle and others, particularly the *Ethics* and the *Rhetoric*. And in those texts—sometimes explicitly, sometimes less directly—there was an engagement with political philosophy, at least, but sometimes political events. I find it hard to see how you could read *Being and Time* neutrally after all that. So what I tried to do is show how *Being and Time* was, in the terms Heidegger had established at that time in his thought, political. It was not an attempt to read back into the text ideas or actions from the 1930s. I think that Heidegger was predisposed to make the kinds of errors he did because of some key failings in his philosophy. I do think the discussion of *Mitsein* and *Miteinandersein* are key to this—how do you think being-with-others, particularly because ideas of society and community are so crucial to how you think politics. Obviously people like Levinas and Jean-Luc Nancy have discussed this too.

I do think that Heidegger's analysis of the *Gestell* and his critique of the politics of calculation more generally, is the key to his answer to the question of how to understand National Socialism. I think it's a very powerful account, and can (and has) been taken forward in many ways, although of course it is missing the ethical dimension. While it's right to criticize Heidegger for that, it's probably a bit too easy. And of course moral critiques of National Socialism are easier than ontological ones. I do think he tried hard to explain, even if perhaps only to himself, what he thought went wrong. The "Letter on Humanism" is a good place to look.

Paul John Ennis: How do you manage to remain so prolific and can you provide us with some advice on the writing process? Do you think that as someone who is not plugged directly into the world of academic philosophy it is easier for you to talk about philosophy is a clear style?

Stuart Elden: I'm really interested in how academics write, in that it's clear that we work in very different ways. I've done a couple of sessions on writing and publishing (from my experience as a journal editor) when I've been a visiting academic in other departments. The key thing is that there is no correct way to write, but ways that work for individuals. The problem is that many people seem to try to write in ways that are not right for them, that are just not working. Personally I try to write every day, even if it is just typing up some notes or work on references. I try not to get too hung up over particular words or formulations; because I go over things so many times that I never think anything I write initially is the final version. For me that's helpful in not getting blocked. I write a lot of "stage directions" into the text –"this link doesn't work"; "need better examples"; "develop" etc. – and I move on. I type all my notes into the computer these days, which helps massively with finding things.

I write a lot, which is partly because most things I read make me want to write about them. So I write comments around the quotes, and build things up. In that sense, a lot of texts emerge – I don't tend to start with word one, and often don't set out to write an article or a book. The book I have coming out later this year, *Terror and Territory*, came about because I wanted to write a piece on the contemporary state of territory to show why I thought the historical study I was doing was worthwhile. What could I say about the "war on terror" from the perspective of territory? That one piece led to another, and soon I had a few articles, some lectures and ideas, which I realized would make a book.

I suppose if there is one piece of advice, it is not to put the writing off too long. I write in part to make sense of what I'm thinking, or what I'm reading. You can always throw it away later. But leaving the writing until you've done all the reading or preparation seems to me to be a problem. That said, I do know people who claim to work that way, and they can "turn on" the writing at that late point. It just doesn't work for me – writing is more of a slow accumulation. I've written some shorter pieces quite quickly, but most pieces are built up very slowly, accretion over a long period of time. The other thing to note is that I work on several things – not quite at once – but in parallel. So the history of territory book has been ongoing for nearly a decade; *Speaking Against Number* has some aspects that are a proper answer to a question Mick Dillon asked me in my PhD viva; I started work on Lefebvre during my PhD but it didn't make the submitted version, and so on. The other thing that is crucial is not to let conference papers sit after you've delivered them. I know of lots of people with "orphaned" papers – ones that they did some work on, maybe presented and received feedback, but never finished. I finish pretty much everything, and tend to tailor speaking invitations to what I want to be writing on. Especially while on a research fellowship, and thus not teaching, I've found it important to keep giving papers at regular intervals, but these days I tend to accept invitations only with conditions: I will speak but this is what I am working on at the moment. If that doesn't fit the event, fine – neither I nor the person inviting me tends to be put out. But it means that I use presentations as means towards the end of writing.

In terms of clarity, I don't know. It's kind of you to say this, though I suspect a lot of people think that I either miss the complexity or needlessly obfuscate! I suppose trying to talk about these ideas in different disciplines, to students, conferences etc. means that you have to work on how you explain things. I remember someone saying to me that if you simplify Hegel too much he's no longer Hegel and I think there is some truth in that. Some of the Anglo-American readings of Heidegger have perhaps been guilty in that sense. But on the other hand, I have a problem with the kinds of philosophers who think you write about a philosopher best by adopting their style. Some of the literature on Derrida for instance…

Thinking about it, *Speaking Against Number* is the book I've written that engages least with issues in geography, although it was the first book I wrote while based in a geography department. It's in a political theory series, some of the work in it was given as lectures in philosophy departments, and I've published on Heidegger in philosophy or political theory journals. There have been some generous reviews from within philosophy. I'd like to think it works on those terms, even though by institutional position I've been outside of philosophy as a discipline.

Paul John Ennis: If you had the chance to give your younger self advice on graduate school what would it be?

Stuart Elden: I guess it's more a piece of information, rather than advice. But it's to say that it can be easy to see established academics as somehow having all the answers, and getting it right all the time. But I don't think that's the case. From my own experience, and as a journal editor, I know that getting referee reports you don't like; being asked to make changes you don't want; and being rejected really does happen to everyone. I know very few people who have never been rejected; and I think sometimes that never being rejected means your work is not challenging established orthodoxies or practices enough. In other words it's safe, mundane, competent but sometimes boring work. Innovative, challenging work often gets a rough ride from established referees. Everyone gets reports they don't like. I can think of maybe one paper to *Society and Space* in my time as editor that has only needed very minor revisions. Most need work, some obviously more than others. It's tough and like all of us you will get down about this. The best way to deal with it is to talk to friends and colleagues. If they are being honest all will have had similar experiences.

Paul John Ennis: What, in your opinion, is the future of post-Continental philosophy?

Stuart Elden: I'm not well qualified to comment on this in general terms. I've been impressed by some recent work. Quentin Meillassoux's *After Finitude* was one of the most remarkable books I've read in a long time, and although I've ventured into print on it, I am still thinking about its implications and challenges. Graham Harman's *Tool Being* was the most challenging and original book on Heidegger in ages. So there are encouraging signs of new voices emerging, rather than just more work from the established people. I do appreciate the work being done to bring into circulation the lecture courses of Heidegger, Foucault and now Derrida, and translations of works are always welcome, but most of the "new" thinkers of the past decade have been already "old". That said, I do think that there are some criminally underrated thinkers, who, largely because they have been poorly served by translation, are almost unknown in the Anglophone world. Eugen Fink, for instance, who served as Husserl's assistant and then worked with Heidegger, wrote a terrific book entitled *Spiel als Weltsymbol—Play as a Symbol of World*—which was slated for translation in 1971, but it never appeared. His work has only really been translated in terms of his relation to better known figures, which is a real shame. Similarly with Kostas Axelos, who like Fink, seems to me to offer much to a philosophy of the world, which would help some of the conceptually weak thinking that runs through globalization. Personally I think it is much more worthwhile that what Jean-Luc Nancy has written on the subject. Sloterdijk, who I mentioned before, is another thinker whose translation is overdue. Fortunately, in his case at least, this is fast being remedied.

I would however venture a few words on the relation between contemporary philosophy and geography. For some time, geography has been engaging with philosophy or theory more broadly. Some very interesting work has been done. But geography's engagement with thinkers has tended to lag behind other disciplines, and to be parasitic on the work of translation, edition and introduction done by others. The exception is Lefebvre, from the initial work of people like David Harvey in getting *The Production of Space* translated, to the work of Elizabeth Lebas and Eleonore Kofman on the *Writings on Cities* collection. More recently Neil Brenner and I have been trying to make other texts available. But this has tended to be unusual. It would be good if geographers took on the work of making available works by thinkers whose work is profoundly relevant to contemporary debates in geography, but also geographical thinkers like Claude Raffestin who work is little known in English. People like Marc Augé and Giorgio Agamben are used by geographers, but thus far it has largely been people in other disciplines who have done the "academic service" work. One of the things I've tried to do as editor of the journal *Environment and Planning D: Society and Space* has been to commission translations. We've had pieces by Balibar, Sloterdijk and Badiou in recent issues, but it is a lot of work. In general terms, I'd like to see geography's engagement with theory aspire to the standards of rigor set by two other areas: work on theory in other disciplines, on the one hand; and geography's own empirical work, on the other.

Interview with Ian Bogost

Paul John Ennis: Can you tell us a little bit about your intellectual background? It seems you've had quite the diverse career so far.

Ian Bogost: I've been interested in both philosophy and computation since a young age. My family didn't own a computer until later than some did in the early 1980s, which meant that my time with computers at school and at friends' houses was more precious, more revered perhaps. I was also interested in literature and the arts for as long as I can remember, and I participated in painting, music, writing, and the like. When I was a teenager I thought I wanted to go into finance, but mercifully I had the opportunity to work in that industry in New York as an intern at 16, a convenient time to discover that I'd rather do anything else. After that experience, I had the sense that I wanted my eventual work life to incorporate and integrate philosophy, the arts, and computation, but I didn't have any idea what that might mean.

When I started undergrad, I felt that I had to choose between them. In retrospect that was probably wrong. But it was the 1990s, and I figured that I could learn as much about computers as I wanted on my own, from colleagues, or in the industry. But where else was I going to learn philosophy? The dot-com boom was perhaps unforeseeable, but I was certain that there would be no ontology boom to mirror it. And internet-connected armchair communities of late-night philosophers weren't a reality, except maybe on USENET. So I made my choice. I'll never forget the experience visiting the undergraduate advisor to change my major from computer science as a freshman: walking down the dark hallway of closed, blue doors, keyboards chattering behind them like. A closed door, a knock, a pause, a silent pass of the form, a quiet signature, a closed door again.

I ended up doing majors in both philosophy and comparative

literature. At the University of Southern California the philosophy department was very Analytical, and the comp lit department very Continental and much focused on critical theory. Comparative literature also let me exercise my interest in literature and the arts, of course, and it forced me to pursue study in several languages, for which I am grateful. I feel now like I got the best of both worlds, philosophically speaking. It turned out I was right about computing or right enough anyway. The World Wide Web was just beginning to reach the public, and Los Angeles was an active center for its commercialization. I worked in the industry through most of undergrad and grad school, building software, websites, and videogames, primarily for use in the entertainment, automotive, and consumer packaged goods industries. I worked insane hours at times and learned how to make systems that real people used. I dealt with a variety of practical if absurd problems, including inadvertently destroying most of Honda's customer database and suffering the arbitrary wrath of action film director Michael Bay. I got my taste of working in big industry and in Hollywood, and I never need to do either of those things again.

Eventually I quit, finished my dissertation, and started a small games studio (called *Persuasive Games*, which later also became the title of my second book) that makes videogames about social and political issues. I was fortunate to have academic and professional advisers willing to support a research project on philosophy and computing – I was ready to give up on the idea of becoming a professor and would have without the intervention of a few important mentors. Still, I'd like to think that by that time I had learned more than a little about how to get my own way from working in the real world of high stakes business. I learned that I would have to forge my own path if I was going to be happy as an intellectual.

My plight seems quaint in retrospect. The faculty gig I landed at Georgia Tech does exactly what I'd hoped I'd be able to do, but never imagined would actually exist: to integrate the liberal arts and computing in a meaningful way. While I sometimes regret not having had a more formal education in computing, formal training can be a burden as much as a benefit. It took me much longer than I might have hoped to reconsider fidelity to early intellectual heroes, while I had no trouble ripping through a variety of computer languages and media without concern. Still, as I watch our hundreds of students make their way through our unique degrees in Computational Media (BS) and Digital Media (MS, PhD), I sometimes wonder if they aren't missing out on the struggles of ossified disciplinarity, or the depth of inquiry possible when one focuses on a single subject. These are the compromises one has to make when doing work that is truly new. A while back, I suggested that the best metaphor for intellectual progress is love, not interdisciplinarity. Something always has to give.

Paul John Ennis: What made you focus on gaming in particular and can you tell us a little bit about the philosophical side of what you do?

Ian Bogost: When we think about computing today, we usually think of networked communications: email, the World Wide Web, blogs, and so forth. Despite their incredible cultural reach and impact, such matters are quite uninteresting uses of the computer. All they do is move bits around through networks, displaying the results in mundane and predictable ways. The real power of computation comes not from digitization and trans-mission, but from procedurality, the machine's ability to accept and execute rule-based behaviors. These behaviors can come together in surprising ways, modeling complex systems of reality or invention.

I'm reasonably interested in games of all sorts, but to me the videogame represents the flowering spring of computational expression: the fertile ground from which machines grow like vines around ideas and artistry. My fascination with videogames arose initially from my interest in computers and art, but it was their tendency to embrace computational procedurality that won me over. Videogames feel like the apotheosis of computing to me, even if they remain cultural underdogs.

Furthermore, videogames draw our attention to the materiality of things. This is not because they are commodities (although that is also true), but because they involve complex assemblages of things at a variety of scales. This is the area of coupling between my media-critical interests in computational media and my philosophical interests in speculative realism. The sphere I have in mind is that of all the objects at work in videogames under the surface, hidden in their "subterranean dimensions," to use Graham Harman's word for it. Consider this: videogames are expressive media experiences that implicate players in their action. But videogames are also comprised of molded plastic controllers, motor-driven disc drives, silicon wafers, plastic ribbons, and bits of data. And they are likewise comprised of subroutines and middleware libraries compiled into byte code or etched onto silicon, cathode ray tubes or LCD displays mated to insulated, conductive cabling, and microprocessors executing machine instructions that enter and exit address buses.

All of these aspects of videogames could be construed as "objects" in Harman's sense of the word: individual beings in themselves, things with a footprint on the world. These sorts of objects are unique to videogames compared to many other sorts of things whose meaning or social power might be observed and studied, like board games or motion pictures or taverns or campfires. But they are especially prevalent in computer artifacts like videogames, much more so than in other forms of human creativity. One might say that the object density in videogames is very high, and that's one reason I am drawn to them. From a philosophical perspective, I find myself thinking about games in perhaps the same way that Žižek thinks about film, or at least an idealized version of it. In the early Žižek, at least, film served as a kind of proof that Lacan could be explained in a reasonably effective way. The subtitle of *Looking Awry* is "An Introduction to Jacques Lacan through Popular Culture," but it could just as easily be reversed, "An Introduction to Popular Culture through Jacques Lacan." In fact, I've often wondered if the latter name better characterizes the book. In any event, I'd like to think that my approach to both philosophy and game studies feedback on one another dialectically.

Paul John Ennis: In a past life you were a Derridean. What made you abandon this path and have you taken any lessons from Derrida into your current area of research?

Ian Bogost: Hopefully this won't seem like a dodge, but I'd like to start this response by citing a much longer answer to a similar question, one I asked myself the day after Derrida died in the autumn of 2004:

...my first public paper on the notion of the digital was presented at a conference with Derrida as the respondent. The entirety of my experience with Derrida's work remains very much bound to this personal meeting, and even more so to the margins of that meeting, the coffee breaks, the conference dinner [at an unassuming Thai restaurant]. ... For me, Derrida personalized philosophy, made me think of it as an activity in which I was personally implicated. Perhaps this is why my experience of Derrida's work is in large part the experience of my own personal memory: that dinner at the Hollywood Thai restaurant; long, bourbon-addled ponderings with friends who remain desperately close, even if we speak seldom; purposely driving over Acts of Literature with a Mazda Miata after a particularly colorful reading group; coming to terms with my objections to deconstruction as I wrote my   dissertation.

As my experience as a student hopefully alludes, there was something of myself that I saw in Derrida's thinking: the idea of an alternative, a neither this nor that. Neither philosophy nor computation, neither Analytic nor Continental, neither professor nor professional, neither *Glas* nor glass noodles, but both, or neither, all at the same time. In this respect, Derrida opened my eyes in ways I will always be grateful for (as I will for the influential American deconstructionists I had the benefit of studying under), but once my eyes were opened, I didn't know what I saw. Nothing. A blank vista. A desert. Why? Deconstruction is superb at setting things in eternal motion, like some wild steampunk apparatus fastened with magnets of opposing poles. And that apparatus is mesmerizing. But beyond enchantment, it offers little direction on what practical steps to take. It is a paperweight. Once things are destabilized, then what? It is poetic and moving to assert, like Samuel Beckett, "I can't go on, I'll go on," but what sort of coward or psychopath would leave his companions stranded there, in the desert, with this useless joke of a compass? Go where, exactly? To do what, precisely? What's the third term, the structure that offers alternative to the *aporia* without reconciling it? Deconstruction can never answer this question, by definition, yet it is where the real work resides.

I found myself confused, and angry. Why did this thoughtful, coherent, generous man write books that verged on the incomprehensible, that did more to isolate philosophy from the world than to fold it back in? Why did those who followed his work seem less rather than more engaged, obsessed with illusion, obfuscation, and repetition? Was it some sort of trick that one had to have the opportunity to meet and converse with Derrida to get an insight into his true nature as a thinker? Was he an illusionist or a fool not to have made such matters clear in his work? Most of all, I found myself confused by those who adopted his thinking in the arts, where they might have actually been formed into word, stone, canvas, celluloid, or plush. But instead, it became standard practice simply to argue that the reconciliation of whatever opposing concepts one might find is "always already impossible," philosophy an eternal Easter egg hunt in search of shiny, cubed ovoids to be worshiped over red wine.

I suppose I am still in part a deconstructionist, motivated by the conflicts between domains. I also suspect that Derrida's obsession with language and close reading, something inherited from Heidegger, invited me to think about philosophy as an engineering problem, to use the words Levi Bryant recently put to it. But I am now motivated to do something about some of those conflicts, in a way that people can understand and use. In this respect, it's hard not to admire Slavoj Žižek, even if I do wish he could throw a party without inviting Hegel.

Paul John Ennis: Would it be possible for you to give an overview of your ideas regarding technology, and if possible can you give us your opinion on Heidegger's views on technology?

Ian Bogost: My basic perspective on technology is that it must be understood on many registers. We cannot simply speak of technology as a domain of human activity and call it moral or corrupt, nor the effects of technology and call them good or bad, nor the form of technological works and call them beautiful or ugly, nor the expressive payload of technological artifacts and call them meaningful or useless. Indeed, we ought not to speak of technology as a category if we can help it, but instead, we ought to see specific technologies as having various material forms and interacting with things, both human and non-human, in specific ways.

In our book on the Atari VCS, *Racing the Beam*, Nick Montfort and I outline one way of engaging with computational creativity that tries to do something like this. We outline five levels that characterize the common focuses of study in digital media:

Reception - focused on the experience of the user.

Interface - focused on the user's relationship to the visible, operable part of a computer system.

Form and Function - focused on the operation and behavior of the program.

Code - focused on the way work is programmed and understood by programmers.

Platform - focused on the abstraction layer beneath code.

Each of these connects to culture and context in specific ways, and in different ways still when combined together into pairs and triads. Very frequently, effective studies of new media will draw from multiple levels of this model. In our work, Nick and I wanted to endorse the platform layer in particular, as both a promising and under-explored aspect of computational scholarship, because we felt it had been ignored the most.

Ours is one model, there could be others. But importantly, it's a model that refuses to take any individual slice through technology as primary: not the social construction of technology (SCOT) perspective that platforms and code are produced solely by human action, not the technological determinist perspective that those two layers set the conditions of interfacing and reception, not the materialist perspective that matters of human labor and capital override all others, not the formalist perspective that operation is king, not the art historical perspective that the visual surface of objects is all that matters, not any of these individually, but not none of them together either. Here I would also resist the temptation to apply a simple model of relation between them, à la Actor-Network Theory. Even a network is too ossified a structure for me when it is constructed only once, in reference to a specific artifact like a dishwasher or a videogame console. An alternate metaphor, perhaps, is a basket of laundry, or a pile of leaves, or a caffe latte. In this regard, I'm more enamored of John Law's notion of a "mess" as a characterization of technological relation.

As for Heidegger, I empathize with the idea that we can embrace neither technofetishism nor luddism. That is to say, technology is neither a fundamental and unquestioned good, its flaws only to be resolved through more technology, or is it a fundamental evil that we can opt-out of. Indeed, the former perspective, which Heidegger expands in the notions of standing-reserve and enframing, is so predominant in some areas of computer science and "geek culture" that it is sometimes tempting to accept the alternative, out in the woods with the blueberries and the chickens. Of course, such a gesture would not help us avoid technology, if we adopt Heidegger's understanding of it.

Still, since I deal largely in computer technology, Heidegger's standing-reserve can be helpful. It can help liberate objects like microprocessors and RJ45 connectors and molded plastic casings from the instrumentality of application, of enframing. One could, perhaps, say that platform studies are an invitation to reconsider enframing in computation. But Heidegger's insistence on total-izing technology as a single whole seems untenable to me, or perhaps just unhelpful. The concept of "world" as a total substance just offers yet another excuse to remain ignorant of specific things, whether they are flint or windmills or hydro-electric plants or videogame consoles. Here I find Marshall McLuhan's invitation to investigate the properties of specific technologies to be liberating and productive... not to mention a hell of a lot clearer!

Paul John Ennis: You are one of the many thinkers today interested in speculative realism. What attracted you to these areas and can you foresee any applications into your own field arising from this engagement?

Ian Bogost: To me, the attraction of object-oriented philosophy seems like a given to any scholar of media interested in the thingness of their objects of study in addition to their production, uses, and meaning. In the case of computing, we've done so little collective historical work on material underpinnings that we now have decades of very active productivity in a variety of domains that have ripened without being picked, so to speak. Yet, save the relatively broad-based approach we can inherit from McLuhan, no good critical approaches exist that would invite questions about the media themselves in addition to the messages they carry (I say "in addition to" because McLuhan does take things too far when he insists that the content of media doesn't matter). In particular, media studies of all kinds have settled on an implicit obsession with various theories of political economy and reception, some interesting and some outmoded, but none of which take "materialism" to mean "realism." I suspected there would be productive connections with object-oriented philosophy, and I remember waiting for Graham Harman's *Tool-Being* to be published in 2002 so I could read it and apply it in my dissertation. It seems that potential conjunction of interest is finally being realized.

The applications are immediate, and they are already taking place. In my case, I am interested in doing object-oriented philosophy in the service of specific classes and instances of objects. The application to game studies and new media studies is already present in spirit, if not always in name, in parts of *Unit Operations* and all of *Racing the Beam*. But I'm also interested in looking beyond those fields, to media and technology studies more broadly. I've begun using the term "pragmatic speculative realism" for this, and I've already done some writing that moves in the direction I have in mind (this work will also mark a more explicit return to the concept of the unit operation). The fundamental question that interests me is how speculative realism can help us address specific objects, like McLuhan does, but without the correlationist burden, without always relating them to human experience. I'm working on a book on this topic now.

Paul John Ennis: Do you think philosophy has somewhat underestimated the influence of the gaming revolution? I noticed whilst browsing your blog that you try to create videogames with political and social messages. Would I be right in assuming that you think, as someone like Žižek might, that games are already in some sense ideological or contain arguments?

Ian Bogost: Yes and no. Or maybe, no and yes. If we look at the history of philosophy – and we don't even have to look very hard – we find frequent engagement with the ideas of game and play (remember that some languages differentiate between "game" and "play" [English, Danish], whereas other's don't [German, French]). In Plato, for example we find an ongoing relationship between play (*paidia*) and education (*paideia*). This is probably most notable in *The Republic*, where play is presented as a primary mode of pedagogy. Indeed, a mode of play is evident all throughout the dialogues, with Socrates constantly goading and challenging his interlocutors. Then of course we have Kant's idea of "free play" in the faculties of imagination, Wittgenstein's language games, the breathing room of Heidegger's *Zeit-Spiel-Raum*, Gadamer's concept of play as a basis for art, and Derrida's frequent use of play as a tenet of deconstruction. There are others I am omitting or forgetting.

There are a few true philosophers of games. The idea of playful seriousness comes up in Johan Huizinga's anthropological take on "Homo Ludens," man the player. Huizinga's belief is that culture writ large (law, art, poetry, language, dance, even philosophy itself) is underwritten by a "play element." McLuhan adopts a belief somewhat compatible with Huizinga's. He gives a place to games in *Understanding Media*, arguing that games extend man's social self. And Roger Caillois offers a classification of games into the categories of *agon* (competition), *alea* (chance), *mimesis* (roleplay), and *ilinx* (vertigo). Much of this work has been ignored or glossed over in philosophy (does any philosopher consider Huizinga a member of the club?). Yet, thinkers in game studies and game design who are very sensitive to these key terms often have succeeded in clarifying and expanding on them from a philosophical perspective, in ways philosophy itself remains oblivious to. For example, I think contemporary game designers Katie Salen and Eric Zimmerman offer the most useful and elegant philosophical definition on play ("free movement within a more rigid structure"), and they do so in a textbook on game design (*Rules of Play*).

Furthermore, philosophy generally fails to treat games as artifacts in their own right—not even in the usual Continental fashion, as "texts" to be "closely read." While he's not considered a philosopher either, it's interesting to note that Marcel Duchamp was much more interested in chess than in painting all throughout his life. When he says things like "Chess can be described as the movement of pieces eating one another" it's hard not to wonder what he would have thought of Pac-Man. Apart from Duchamp, another artist/thinker of the 20th century looked beyond the quasi-games of the dadaists and surrealists: Guy Debord. NYU (New York University) professor Alex Galloway has recently re-implemented Debord's unusual boardgame *Kriegspiel* in a videogame edition, and he has written a definitive article about the game and its relation to Debord's thinking to accompany it.

Speaking of Pac-Man, as for videogames, almost all aspects of contemporary culture have underestimated the role these artifacts play in the contemporary world. So it's easy to say that philosophy has too. That's beginning to change across the board, and philosophy seems to be coming along for the ride, even if slowly. As of autumn 2009, there have been four "Philosophy of Computer Games" conferences, as well as two collections of works drawn from those events. Miguel Sicart, a professor at the IT University Copenhagen, has published a book called *The Ethics of Computer Games*. As I described above, much of my work is drawn from my background in philosophy. But all of these examples are those of videogame scholars who have imported philosophy as a tool. Philosophers seem to think as much about videogames as they do about freight logistics, small-batch bourbon distillation, lightning storms, and NASCAR racing. Yet, these things, like videogames, touch the lives of millions. They are not hypothetical nor are they prurient. They are a part of the world worthy of serious consideration by philosophy as much as by cultural studies.

As for arguments and ideologies, indeed they are present in games. One of my books, *Persuasive Games*, is about this very matter. In that book I advance a new form of rhetoric, which I call procedural rhetoric. Oral and written rhetoric describe, and visual rhetoric depicts, but procedural rhetoric models. Procedural systems are rhetorically powerful because they can simulate behaviors; they can make claims about the way things work. Computation is an example of a medium that is fundamentally procedural, and videogames are the apotheosis of computational procedurality.

But, as you anticipate, not all procedural claims are arguments; some represent ideologies which, by definition, remain unseen to their designers and perhaps their players. I devote a chapter to ideology in the book, but my favorite example comes from the game *America's Army*, which was created by the US Army as a publicity and recruiting tool. It's a multiplayer game, in which players, grouped into teams, compete against one another. In each mission one team plays as the US Army and another plays a group of guerrilla insurgents. Each has a mission objective, and the team who meets it wins.

Here's the thing: both teams think they are the US Army. Their characters wear army uniforms, and they see their opponents as insurgents. The Army did this because, well, it's a game about being in the army, and it tries to simulate the rules of engagement and other aspects of army life. Of course, this design also exposes a fundamental ideology of American military opposition: the enemy is just the same as we are, except he is evil. There's no complexity of history, no collision of different worlds, just two sides, one good and one wicked. Speaking of Žižek once again, I've had a silent fear for some time that he might someday discover videogames, and then there goes the neighborhood. In a 2007 interview he claimed to play military videogames "compulsively," but a hobby, even a blood sport, doesn't a study make. He's got film already, after all, that old, tired medium of the 20th century. He wouldn't want to come out and play.

Paul John Ennis: If you had the chance to give your younger self advice on graduate school what would it be?

Ian Bogost: First, I'd want to remind myself that the struggle against one's mentors is a natural, even a desirable thing. The job of the graduate student is to outlast the benign oppression of foundational thinkers in order to move beyond them. For every graduate student, this sensation eventually manifests as infantilism, the sense that one is like a teenager held back by oppressive and deluded parents. This is a fruitful angst and it should be applied toward productivity rather than *ennui*. In general, most graduate students would do well to eschew the familiar tune of malaise in favor of something else—anything else: music, television, and astronomy, whatever. As a vital corollary, I'd want to remind myself that true innovation in a field requires forging one's own path. This may sound like a trite aphorism, but it's not. A sense of ease, of facile progress through known terrain, is a sure sign that one's work is doomed to the oblivion of sameness. The most important and potentially successful work is that which struggles to find a place for itself, but persists through the determination and stubbornness of its creator.

An advisor of mine once told me that the students who do best in graduate school are those who are driven to answer a particular question, resolved to answer it no matter what obstacles might arise. That seems right, and it sure sounds good. But there's an upshot to determination: sustainability. Being smart and committed is not enough. Doing the work alone is not enough. One also has to figure out how to find—or more likely, how to create—a situation in which that work is possible. As someone who was trained in the humanities but worked for many years in business, I find no particular inconsistency in having to account for the material, social, and structural under-pinnings of one's work. But strangely, much of modern academia rests on the weird belief that the ideas are enough. Ideas are lovely, but they are fragile flowers, not bedrock. We have to build a shelter for them, and students would do well to learn early that they will need to become masons as well as gardeners.

Paul John Ennis: What, in your opinion, is the future of post-Continental philosophy?

Ian Bogost: I think the future of post-Continental philosophy will exist in productive conversations, as an amphibious ferry across various rivers, roads, and meadows. I don't simply mean to rename the well-trod path of interdisciplinarity, but to suggest that philosophy is re-entering the world in a different way from its predecessors. Continental philosophy has long prided itself on its purported coupling to the material world, mostly through a particular sense of political action. For better or worse, that typically falls in the wake of May '68, a group of ideas that Peter Starr has given the apt name "logics of failed revolt." Starr traces this dynamic in France until the 1976 abandonment of Leninism, but it is clear that an idealized attitude of leftist reform continues to pervade applications of Continental philosophy. This is partic-ularly ironic in the United States, where I am based, since the decades since '68 have simultaneously hosted the massive growth of Continental philosophy and the wholesale rejection of socialist politics in any form.

One of the common gripes Continentalists have with speculative realism amounts to a perception of apoliticism. Yet, the external debates about public life that underwrote much of Continental thought at its origins transformed into internal debates about processes and institutions. Politics became a euphemism for posturing. I think those days are ending. To me, one of the appeals of the new realism is its desire to return to "the great outdoors," to use Quentin Meillassoux's term for it. Part of this process implies a new anti-humanism, a focus on the entire world, and not just particular human experiences of it. But another part implies a different responsibility to the world, to a larger world. I take seriously the charge of the public intellectual, and I'd like that name to refer seriously to real people and real things, and all of them, or as many of them as possible. In this respect, I wonder if the future of philosophy might not bear some similarity to what we once called natural philosophy, full of wonder and curiosity rather than woe and dread.

Interview with Levi R. Bryant

Paul John Ennis: Can you tell us a little bit about your background, and formative influences?

Levi Bryant: I came to philosophy around the age of fourteen or fifteen, after going through a very difficult time in my life. Heidegger, Kant, Spinoza, Descartes, Husserl, and Whitehead came like bolts of lightning to me, allowing me to orient my life around a set of questions and issues. In graduate school I suppose my three mentors were Andrew Cutrofello, Adrian Peperzak, and Patricia Huntington. Andrew Cutrofello taught me to be curious and interested in all philosophical movements and to approach philosophy creatively and eclectically, being unafraid to experiment and "cross-wires." As a dissertation director he was hands off and gave me the freedom to explore my own project without micromanaging it. Adrian Peperzak taught me the art of close reading and engagement with the history of philosophy. Finally, Patricia Huntington instilled in me the sense that philosophy is not simply an academic or scholarly exercise, but should always have a dimension of existential authenticity to it, bound up with questions of who you are and the social and political milieu in which you're embedded.

It is difficult to articulate a precise list of formative influences as I tend to read very widely. Philosophically I am deeply indebted to Lucretius, Spinoza, Heidegger, Whitehead, and Deleuze. Bruno Latour has, of course, had a decisive impact on my thought, but I also find myself perpetually returning to the rather obscure German sociologist Niklas Luhmann who first introduced me to systems theory and autopoietic theory. My conception of objects is thoroughly indebted to autopoietic theory and dynamic systems theory. Lacan, Freud, and Žižek are everywhere in my thought and had a central influence on my own intellectual development. I even practiced as a Lacanian analyst for a time. I suppose that these thinkers taught me to be suspicious of totalizing systems, the desire for completeness, and to make room for the role that the "unthought" plays in thought. In the sciences I have always had a love for biology, and am particularly sympathetic to the work of Gould and developmental systems theorists such as Susan Oyama. I owe Alberto Toscano a debt of gratitude for introducing me to her work through his *Theatre of Production*.

Gould's lengthy masterpiece, *The Structure of Scientific Revolution*, is far more than a treatise on evolutionary theory. It is a veritable tome of ontological theory. What makes Gould's work so fascinating is that so much of it revolves around questions of what constitutes individuals. So you get individuals at all levels of scale: genes, cells, organisms, species, genera, and so on. As a consequence, you can have individuals or what I call objects within objects and selection takes place at all these levels. By contrast, the developmental systems theorist emphasizes the inseparability of organism-environment relations, showing how it is not simply genes that determine the organism, but rather how you have a whole cascade of irreversible processes presiding over the development of an organism without one factor, such as genes, determining the final outcome. Genes are treated as one factor among many. No doubt this insight has had a deep impact on the formulation of my ontic principle which states that there is no difference that does not make a difference. What I try to think is the interaction of all these differences from diverse domains and the role they play in the production of the final outcome or actualized entity.

Finally, in the domain of history, I am particularly influenced by the work of Ferdinand Braudel. Braudel wrote a marvelous multi-volume history of the emergence of capitalism entitled *Capitalism and Civilization*. What makes this work so remarkable is that it does not narrate history from the standpoint of ideas or great events or of great men and women, but from the standpoint of everyday life. What you thus get are these elaborate discussions of what homes were like, what sorts of food people ate, the various forms of grains, meats, and cheeses produced and how they were produced, technologies used, disease epidemiologies and so on. Braudel gives a real sense of the "material infrastructure", what he calls "material history" that influences life and social organization and therefore fundamentally shifts your understanding of why social organizations have the form or pattern they do.

Paul John Ennis: Your next book includes a proposal for your own realist ontology. Can you give us a sneak preview of what you have in mind?

Levi Bryant: *The Democracy of Objects* is still very much in its preliminary stages, so I can only vaguely sketch what I hope to develop. Perhaps the key question of the book is "what is the relation of relation and relata?" Since Locke the old substances have fallen into disrepute, whereas since Hegel the world has increasingly come to be understood as consisting of nothing but relations. In my view Harman has made a significant contribution to philosophy in trying to resurrect substances, arguing that without any autonomous substances the world becomes unintelligible, evaporating into networks of relations that relate nothing, and that we are thus unable to explain how change is possible without positing autonomous substances as nothing is left in reserve within these networks of relations.

The Democracy of Objects thus seeks a flat ontology – an ontology where all objects are on equal footing – that redeems the category of substance. Returning to Locke, the category of substance falls into ill repute because when we strip away all the qualities of an object to get at that which endures through time as identical or the same despite change, we're left with nothing at all. This will later lead Kant to claim, for example, that substance isn't in the things themselves but is rather a category imposed by mind on the matter of intuition. With substance ontologists preceding Locke, I agree that substances or objects are not their qualities. Qualities change, but the object remains the same. However, I do not concede that substance is a bare substratum without structure or organization. Rather, I argue that sameness of objects or substances throughout time lies in their structure as a system of attractors defining a phase space that can be actualized in a variety of ways. In developing this thesis, I draw heavily on the work of Zubiri, Deleuze, and DeLanda. In a nutshell, an attractor is a point towards which a system tends under determinate conditions. For example, the bottom of a bowl is an attractor for a marble rolling up and down the side of the bowl, and the richness of the blue of my coffee mug is an attractor state for the mug under certain lighting conditions (the mug appears black under different lighting conditions). The phase space of an object, by contrast, is all possible states it can enter into at the qualitative level.

Substance, I argue, is this structure of attractors or what Deleuze called a "multiplicity". Under this construal, qualities turn out to be actualized points in phase space. In this way, I'm able to undermine the distinction between substance and quality that has vexed so much philosophy since Locke, but I am also able to abolish the distinction between accident and essence insofar as qualities are actualized as a result of the affects or attractor structure of objects. We even get the beginnings of a realist epistemology in this conception of substance insofar as part of knowing substance involves placing them in differential fields that allow attractors of substances to manifest themselves. In this regard, philosophy has conceived the activity of knowing in far too passive terms, privileging the gaze or regard of objects, ignoring how we must grock with objects to discover their nature or the differences they contribute to the world.

The Democracy of Objects will approach objects from three interrelated perspectives. After introducing the principles of onticology, it will explore the endo-relational structure of objects or their endo-consistency in terms of their structure as systems of attractors. I refer to this analysis of object qua object, independent of any of its relations to other objects as the "onticological Analytic". The second part of the book will explore exo-relations or networks of objects in relation to one another. Here I am heavily indebted to Deleuze and Guattari and Latour. Clearly many of the conditions under which objects actualize a point in phase space are dependent on the object's relation to other objects. The second part will thus explore these relations of evocation among objects, but will also examine those conditions under which objects come to form a system or organization amongst themselves that becomes self-sustaining and operationally closed from other objects. I refer to this second part as the "onticological dialectic" to emphasize that it is concerned with relations among objects. Finally, the third part of the book will examine the genesis of objects. Under certain conditions objects are pushed into new basins of attraction, generating new objects that have a substantial autonomy of their own. This portion of the book I refer to as the "ontological deduction" insofar as it accounts for the formation of objects. I think there will be plenty in this book to excite the technology, media, social and political, and ecological theorists.

Paul John Ennis: Can you tell us a little bit about what attracted you to speculative realism and further what you think its future prospects might be?

Levi Bryant: As I have argued elsewhere, speculative realism doesn't really exist. Rather, it is a generic term for a group of thinkers that advocate very different ontologies and epistemologies, and who are often opposed to one another. Generally there are only two features that unite these thinkers: a commitment to some variant of realism, and a refusal to privilege the world-human correlate. My way to speculative realism occurred very gradually. *Larval Subjects* started as a blog devoted almost entirely to Deleuze, Badiou, and Lacan. In particular, I was trying to figure out how to synthesize my Deleuzian ontological commitments with my Lacanianism. Back in 2006 the blog was still quite scholarly in flavor, focusing on the careful exposition of these thinkers and working out knots in my understanding of their thought.

However, it could be said that the more recent shifts in my thought have very much been a product of my experience with blogging. Blogging is genuinely a new form of writing, thinking, and intellectual engagement when done properly. This point and blogging's difference can be illustrated in terms of evolutionary theory. One of the primary ways in which speciation takes place is through geographical isolation. Two populations of a single species come to be reproductively isolated for some reason or other and as time passes their phenotypes diverge and the respective populations become homogenous. It is really no different in traditional academia. You talk to people who share the same interests as you, you attend conferences devoted to your particular issue or thinker, you publish in journals devoted to your privileged thinker, and you read texts on your privileged thinker or problem. These are all forms of geographical isolation that lead to "academic speciations".

This sort of isolation isn't operative in the world of blogging. While you certainly encounter specialists in your particular area, you also encounter thinkers from entirely different disciplines, practices, and orientations and you have to find a way to engage with them that doesn't assume the daunting scholarly apparatus of your particular thought-framework. You encounter all sorts of characters like satirists and trolls, but also housewives, people in business, activists, people from different disciplines and philosophical orientations, artists, politicians and all the rest. A good deal of my early work was devoted to trying to fit Deleuze into a correlationist mould, and focused heavily on the signifier and the analysis of cultural artifacts and formations along Žižekian lines. However, in the process of working through these issues I encountered other bloggers such as Nick Srnicek, Reid Kane, Ben Woodard, Taylor Adkins, N. Pepperell, Anthony Paul Smith, and others who were suddenly talking about this strange new beast, "speculative realism". They were referencing unfamiliar names like Quentin Meillassoux, Ray Brassier, Ian Hamilton Grant, and Graham Harman. Much of this seemed to resonate with the direction I was striving to take Deleuze and Badiou in, so I began reading their works.

During this time I was also having intense conversations with the literary, media, and technology theorist Melanie Doherty. She was always emphasizing the role that technology and media technologies play in forming various types of social relations. Well! My signifiers certainly weren't adequate to theorizing or thinking this dimension of reality as a technology is not simply signifiers, so I began to feel a growing disquiet with the adequacy of semiotic approaches to the world. When I finally got around to reading Meillassoux's *After Finitude* it blew my hair back. As the old expression goes, "the scales fell from my eyes" and I realized that I would need to rework my ontology. Filled with excitement, I contacted Nick Srnicek and proposed *The Speculative Turn*, as I knew that he was far more familiar with speculative realism than me, and also that he was well disposed towards Deleuze. Initially the collection was conceived as a sort of realist Deleuzian rejoinder to certain critiques of his thought from other speculative realists. The project exploded from there. We were shocked by the enthusiasm and excitement it generated among those we approached to contribute. Graham Harman, especially, was deeply excited and we struck up a very intense philosophical email exchange. Where our positions started out somewhat opposed to one another, I came out the other side as an advocate of object-oriented ontology, though in an orientation different from Graham's.

My hope, of course, is that interest in speculative realism will continue to grow. Right now we have an entire generation of emerging thinkers – and you will be hearing their names soon all over the place, I suspect – who seem very dissatisfied with the philosophical milieu they've inherited. There's a very real sense in which the possibilities of Continental philosophy have exhausted themselves and the time for something new has arrived. This exhaustion isn't simply to be located in the dearth of research possibilities in academia afforded by traditional orientations of Continental thought, but more importantly by the situation we face in the world today. Philosophical approaches driven by the primacy of the human-world correlate just aren't very useful in thinking our historical moment, or phenomena surrounding the new technology, the ecological crisis, the new developments in the sciences, and the new economics. We need conceptual tools that will allow us to more effectively think these things. The signifier and lived experience, while crucial components, just don't do this. However, should speculative realism continue to grow, I suspect that we'll witness the emergence of divergent orientations of realist thought that enter into debate with one another. In particular, look for debates to emerge between object-oriented strains of speculative realism and materialist strains.

Paul John Ennis: You mention the word "ontic" from time to time: what do you think about Heidegger's ontology, and in particular, his supposed denigration of the ontic? Do you think Deleuze and Badiou have supplanted Heidegger with regards to ontological matters? Or do you think there is still something useful to Heidegger's analysis? Or to put it another way are we in a definitively post-Heideggerian age?

Levi Bryant: My philosophical work actually began with Heidegger and I went to Loyola of Chicago to study with Thomas Sheehan. In particular, I've always been fascinated with Heidegger's account of disclosedness and I think this shows through in certain elements of my own account of objects. Since

I understand myself to be doing ontology, I do not understand my use of the term "ontic" as being opposed to ontology. From a phenomenological point of view, my use of the term "ontic" or my characterization of my ontology as "onticology" can simply be taken as a radicalization of the imperative to return to the things themselves. If I am critical of Heidegger it is simply because I believe that he privileges the human-world relation too much. I think being gets along just fine without man as its shepherd and I do not think beings need to be sheltered in language.

With Whitehead, I don't think philosophies are ever refuted only abandoned. Nor do I think Heidegger's sun has set. I suspect that Deleuze will continue to inspire interest because he developed so many conceptual tools appropriate to our time. I'm less certain of how Badiou's thought will age. I think one thing that determines whether or not a philosophy has lasting power lies in whether or not it creates work for others, both at the interpretive level and at the level of generating new research projects. Badiou's thought, brilliant as it is, just does not seem to afford much work for others. It is difficult to see, however, how Heidegger could be supplanted any time soon. On the one hand, I suspect Harman's work will continue to inspire interest in Heidegger. On the other hand, I think philosophical texts are a bit like holograms. That is, we view them differently with historical circumstances. Rather than abandoning Heidegger, I suspect that certain themes in his thought will come to be accentuated and that others will fall into the darkness.

Paul John Ennis: You state on your blog that you used to be a Lacanian psychoanalyst and interest in Lacan has sky rocked in the past few years due to the work of Slavoj Žižek. Can you tell us a little about the potential benefits of psychoanalysis for philosophy, philosophers, and philosophical thinking? Does Lacan have an effect on your understanding of ontology (as it clearly does on Žižek)? Would it be possible for you to give us some kind of Lacanian insight into Heidegger (no matter how superficial)?

Levi Bryant: I think it is always important to be cautious when giving a psychoanalytic account of the motives that lead one to hold a particular position because such approaches border on the *ad hominem* and ignore the arguments that might be in favor of that position. Freud, for example, gives all sorts of reasons pertaining to desire as to why people believe in God, but his analysis, in no way undermines the existence of God. To do that you would need another sort of argument. In other words, it's entirely possible that everything Freud says about why people are led to belief in God is true, and God nonetheless exists. I think those that practice psychoanalytic critical theory sometimes forget this.

Nonetheless, I do think that psychoanalysis can be of great value in helping philosophers to recognize blind spots in their discourse and philosophical practice. Indeed, Lacan argued that for any discourse to establish itself, it must repress or exclude some element so as to achieve internal consistency. With this repression, of course, there is always a return of the repressed that plagues the discourse in the form of a symptom. Lacan always claimed that philosophy is the discourse of the master, which is to say that it is a discourse that disavows the split in the subject and strives to achieve mastery by unifying the slave's knowledge under a master-signifier transforming it into a smooth conceptual system that claims to be a totality and to be complete. We can certainly see this notion of a sovereign and transparent subject without split in Descartes and even Husserl, but I also think this conception of the subject is ubiquitous in the practice of many philosophers. Thus, while the contemporary thinker – including the psychoanalytically inflected thinker – might give lip service to how the subject is split, going so far as to make it the central thesis of their entire system of thought, they nonetheless proceed in practice as if they were sovereign masters capable of surveying the totality. Really this is a variation of the famous Socratic thesis that the source of our tragedy lies in believing that we know when we do not.

Symptoms of this can be detected all over the place. Thus, those who have been influenced by Lacan often approach popular culture, political events, and various cultural artifacts as if they had the interpretive master-key that lays everything bare to the eye that wishes to know. In this way, texts no longer have the capacity to surprise them as readers as they're already looking for mere exemplifications of their theory. I think, despite all its talk of free play, deconstruction has fallen into a similar cul-de-sac. As Žižek somewhere observes, deconstruction often functions as a sort of metalanguage, such that the reader always knows in advance what he is going to find. To be sure, the text is deconstructed, but along the lines of a pre-delineated code or pattern.

Calls for a critical stance also strike me as suffering from a similar desire for mastery. They would like to know before they know, determining the conditions under which knowledge, for example, is possible, thereby saving themselves the trouble of going through the process of arriving at knowledge as a result. This can be seen as a defense against the aleatory nature of the world that resists our drive to represent it. Similarly, it is today seen as the height of naiveté to actually advocate for a particular position. Rather, one is to be critical of all positions, showing how they are all secretly about something else. In many respects, this resembles the attitude of the obsessional that is perpetually preparing without ever doing anything. In this way, the obsessional is able to disguise his split or incompleteness by never engaging with the world. In my view, philosophical practice can be assisted by becoming more aware of these psychic structures and their role as defenses.

I certainly wouldn't characterize my ontology as Lacanian, though I have been deeply influenced by Lacan. My practice as an analyst or my experience in the clinic had a tremendous impact on my thought. What I encountered in the clinic, I think, was the real. Nothing works in the clinic as it does in theory. You're never quite sure what is going on with your patient and each interpretive intervention you make carries a risk. A simple repetition of a patient's phrase, for example, can lead to them suddenly quitting their job and ending their relationship. This is something advocates of psychoanalytic theory in relation to texts and cultural artifacts never really encounter, I think. Texts do not talk back. You can make of them largely what you would like. This is not the case in the clinic. Just when you think you've gotten things figured out the patient's desire shifts elsewhere and you're in for new surprises.

Additionally, what you discover in the clinic is that people are absolutely different. We go about our day to day business thinking others think like us, that they share our desires, that they share our values; in short that we exist in a common, shared world, but what you discover is that this isn't the case at all. I think a lot of theory and life is organized around repressing this difference. After all, we'd all go mad were we constantly aware of how different others are from all of us. We wouldn't be able to anticipate the impact of our words or actions on anyone. At any rate, psychoanalysis taught me that theories and concepts are not reality laid bare, but rather are more like instruments and lenses. In the clinic, psychoanalytic concepts draw your attention to certain things, make you cognizant of certain things that you might otherwise not notice, but they do not lay bare the truth of your patient. That is something that is only revealed – if at all; it's the patient that comes to know, not the analyst after all; the analyst is just a midwife – through long engagement. Often clinical experience contradicts these concepts and calls for the entire remaking of analysis. This lesson significantly transformed my attitude towards philosophy and what it is about.

Beyond my experience of the clinic, I would say that Lacan's account of sexuation, discourse, and the real also had a decisive impact on my ontology. In one way or another, all of these dimensions of Lacanian thought teach that there is no One, that there is no metalanguage, and that the Whole is not. These are lessons at the heart of my flat ontology.

I am not sure what Lacanian insight I can give into Heidegger's thought. The case of Heidegger is strange because in certain respects Lacan and Heidegger are so close. As I'm sure you know, Heidegger was a tremendous influence on Lacan's own thought. For example, Lacan's concept of time and especially the phenomenon of *après-coup* comes straight out of Heidegger's account of time and the manner in which we build our past out of the manner in which we project our future. This is very close to Lacan's understanding of desire retfoactively rewriting the past and is crucial to how analysis shifts the symptom in treatment. Yet while Heidegger, like Lacan, everywhere seems to recognize the destitution of the subject, he still seems to have this underlying desire for identity and mastery. His famous hostility towards technology and science is reflective, I think, of a horror at destitution, for in modern science and technology we are no longer masters in our own house. Objects attain the power to "speak" and surprise rather than being mere vehicles of our aims and intentions, and technology has all sorts of unanticipated consequences that, as Donna Haraway noted, transform our very nature. There's a very real sense in which we have become elements in machines rather than users of machines. Likewise, his poetic celebration of Black Forest peasants is reflective of a desire for identity and meaning. I thus think there are two Heideggers. There is the Heidegger that went very far in the deconstruction of ontotheology, presence, and what I like to call the "little demiurge" or the sovereign subject, but there is also this other Heidegger that seems to perpetually recoil from this destitution, striving to discover some new ground, meaning, or identity. This has led to a lot of mischief both in his own life and in subsequent engagements with his work. For example, technology studies have been pushed back a great deal as a result of his moralizing and luddite attitude towards enframing.

Paul John Ennis: You seem to be the first to have noticed a link between speculative realism and aesthetics. Can you elaborate upon this? This may come from my ignorance of Deleuze, but does this insight come from your background in Deleuze, and if so can you tell us a little bit about the influence of Deleuze on the overall formation of your thinking?

Levi Bryant: The link I see between aesthetics and speculative realism arises from my background in Deleuze, Whitehead, and Nietzsche. In *Difference and Repetition* Deleuze asserts that his transcendental empiricism re-unites the two sundered halves of the aesthetic. There is, on the one hand, the sense of the aesthetic coming from Kant as a theory of sensibility in the first critique. On the other hand, there is the sense of the aesthetic as a theory of art or the beautiful. In claiming that his transcendental empiricism re-unites the two halves of the aesthetics, I take it that Deleuze is proposing a post-Darwinian theory of sensibility where our receptive faculties are themselves the result of an artistic creation. This is something I've taken with me ever since and is one of the reasons I've been hostile to the Kant of the *Critique of Pure Reason* and functionalist models of mind such as we find in Fodor. In short, they do not do justice to the creative formation of the mind.

In the realm of aesthetic theory, aesthetics has been approached in two ways as well. On the one hand, aesthetics is treated as the theory of artistic judgment. This, for example, is what Kant undertakes in the third Critique. We have the object and the question is how judgments of taste regarding the beauty of the object are possible. It is the spectator theory of art. On the other hand, we have aesthetics as the theory of artistic production. Here the accent isn't on judgment or beauty, but on creation. This is the aesthetic theory we get in Nietzsche and Deleuze, where the emphasis is always on the creation of something. When I discussed the role of aesthetics in ontology, a lot of people expressed concern that this would return us back to a human-centered conception of the real. However, I think this only holds if aesthetics is situated in terms of judgment. Where aesthetics is situated in terms of production and creation, the field of the aesthetic expands vastly, embodying everything from artistic production, to biological speciation, to the formation of solar systems as all of these are processes where the new is being created. The aesthetic becomes a dimension of being itself and objects come to be seen as creations. Whitehead was especially attentive to this ontological and realist orientation of aesthetics. For Whitehead every object is a sort of striving for its optimal aesthetic form.

Paul John Ennis: You seem to read widely in the sciences, but particularly in biology. Is this purely a Deleuzian influence or do you think today philosophers need to be, at the very least, acquainted with developments in the sciences?

Levi Bryant: I wouldn't say that philosophers need to be acquainted with developments in the sciences, but rather that philosophy always needs its others in order to think. In my view, philosophical thought always occurs in and through an encounter with the other or non-philosophy. These others can be art, engineering, love, political revolution, harrowing defeat, programming, environmental work, ethnographic field work, or whatever else you might like. What is important is that there be some encounter with otherness that provokes the thought in the thinker and leads to the question what is reality? For me this encounter has consisted in moving continuously while growing up, the Lacanian clinic, love, and my encounters with science and scientists. I think this is one of reasons that our greatest philosophers and theorists are very seldom professional philosophers. The best philosophical work of the last century has been done outside of philosophy in sociology departments, literature departments, media studies departments, etc. These people are encountering the real in a way that provokes the development of theory. We seldom see philosophical innovation coming from within philosophy departments themselves because these are places where philosophy has been divested of its others and therefore is only able to comment on texts and highly codified problems that have evolved into language games. The very idea of the "professional philosopher" is very strange and only emerged, really, with Hegel. Those philosophers that we all celebrate from the seventeenth century, for example, were all outside of philosophy and devoted primarily to other practices in their day to day life. I suppose, then, that if philosophy needs anything today it is others.

Paul John Ennis: If you had your chance to give your younger self advice on graduate school, what would it be?

Levi Bryant: The best advice I can give to graduate students and aspiring academics is to get involved. Too many of us labor over projects in isolation, never revealing them to anyone else until finally, at long last, they are masterpieces ready for publication. I think this is a tremendous mistake both in terms of prospects for professional success and intellectually. Attending conferences, talking to other academics, participating on discussion lists, and blogging all create countless opportunities and assist in your intellectual development. Nor should this engagement be restricted to established academics. Remember,

79

the people you're talking to will very likely be your colleagues some day. Years later, much to your surprise, you might just find a request to contribute an article or a paper for a conference from someone you haven't talked to for years but who remembers your engagement in some out of the way place. This has happened to me often.

Second, learn how to disagree without being disagreeable and avoid being a "scholar" outside your publications. If you participate publicly in an abusive and ugly manner, this will not only be remembered by the recipient of your abuse, but also by those witnessing the exchange. Don't close doors for yourself because you couldn't resist personalizing the discussion or making it contentious. It is amazing how one indelicate charge of making "strawmen" or "being naïve" can close down all sorts of subsequent opportunities. Similarly, there is something insufferable about the "scholar" who has every minute quote at their fingertips and tries to make all discussion about the intricacies of their pet figure. Learn how to discuss philosophy at the level of issues rather than figures, respect other research orientations, and avoid trying to turn philosophical discussions into textual debates. Save the scholarship for the books and articles you're writing and resist the urge to show off. A list of references, for example, is not a conversation and expecting your interlocutor to remember every minor detail of the person you're dissertating on is unreasonable and obnoxious.

Paul John Ennis: What, in your opinion, is the future of post-Continental philosophy?

Levi Bryant: With Bergson I will plead that if I knew the future of post-Continental philosophy I would be writing it. However, I take it that because the interaction of objects always produces new and unexpected objects, predictions about the future are a fool's game. I will, however, say that I am hopeful. In my view Continental thought— and, for that matter, Anglo-American thought – is emerging from a period of self-reflection that unfolded over the course of the last century. With the success of the sciences, as well as the emergence of the social sciences, I believe that philosophy suffered a sort of crisis of identity, such that it no longer knew what its place was within the academy. Paraphrasing Kant with Freud, we could say that philosophy suffered a wound to its narcissism, recollecting a time when it believed itself to be "queen of the sciences".

This crisis led to a number of postures. We got versions of philosophy that attempted to imitate the sciences or turn themselves into sciences as in the case of Husserl and much of Anglo-American thought. We got other postures that tried to show how philosophy is foundational to the sciences, even though the scientists seemed not to care and to proceed merrily in their "dogmatism" without requiring the authorization of philosophers. We got variants of philosophy that took up the Marxist messianic torch of transforming the world. Finally, we got variants of philosophy that often don't look like philosophy at all, but which consisted in combing over the texts of the philo-sophical tradition and striving to preserve that tradition against the new barbarian hordes living in forgetfulness of the past. All of these postures, I believe, were reactions to a crisis of the identity of the philosopher and the place of philosophy.

Today, it seems, that something is changing and that, like a frozen river, cracks are beginning to show. If Badiou arrived as such a breath of fresh air, then this was because he dared to think, to propose a metaphysic, to speak of truth, in a context where all of this had largely disappeared. Regardless of whether one endorses Badiou's ontology, the simple act of proposing an ontology and of speaking of truth seemed to create an opening where thought was possible again. In the wake of this, everywhere we seem to see thinkers turning away from engagement that is primarily devoted to the analysis of texts, of the canon, and turning towards the world. In the first paragraph of *Being and Time*, Heidegger speaks of a "battle of the giants concerning being". Yet *Being and Time* did not seem to spark this battle. Today, it seems, we are witnessing such rumblings. Speculation seems to have become possible again and, for whatever reason, the world seems to be thrusting itself upon theorists as worthy of thought. Once again, philosophy seems to be discovering its others.

Interview with Adrian Ivakhiv

Paul John Ennis: Heidegger has long been considered a major philosophical source for environmental and deep ecological ideas. As somebody attuned to that world can you tell us whether that is a mistaken or superficial understanding on the part of Heideggerians?

Adrian Ivakhiv: There is a strong resonance between Heideggerian thinking and deep ecology (or biocentrism). Many of the influential thinkers associated with the deep ecology movement – Arne Naess, Bill Devall, George Sessions, and Neil Evernden, among others – refer to Heidegger at least in passing, and some, like Evernden and Dolores LaChapelle, have worked with Heideggerian ideas more extensively. Ecophilosophers, including Michael Zimmerman, Bruce Foltz, Laura Westra, and Ingrid Leman-Stefanovic, while not necessarily identifying themselves as "deep ecologists," have brought a fair bit of refinement into the environmental application of Heideggerian concepts. The key Heideggerian ideas that have been taken up within biocentric writing are his critique of technology, i.e. its essence as *Gestell*, the disclosure of things as raw material for human use, and his notion of *Gelassenheit*, generally conveyed as "letting things be."

Heidegger's later writings on poetry, art, and language as the "house of being" have also influenced a certain subset of ecocritics (ecologically oriented literary and cultural critics) including Jonathan Bate, Greg Garrard, and Kate Rigby. That said, Heidegger has been critiqued (rightly, I think) for a residual anthropocentrism, and his involvement with Nazism has negatively affected the extent of interest in his philosophy among environmentalists. In the end, I would say his philosophy has been one among several sources, often taken up somewhat superficially (as in the influential *Deep Ecology* text co-written by Devall and Sessions in the 1980s) though at least occasionally with a fair bit of rigor, but it has been a crucial one only for a limited subgroup of biocentric thinkers, and less so for activists. Deep ecology, it should be mentioned, evolved in constant conversation with the activities of movement activists, including the radical wilderness activism of Dave Foreman and other founders of *Earth First!* and the more broadly political work of later *Earth First!* activists and related groups. Its theoretical positions have also been refined and developed in dialogue with those of social ecologists, ecofeminists, postmodern and poststructural ecologists, pragmatist ecophilosophers, more mainstream rights- or virtue-based environmental ethicists, and perhaps most closely with Buddhist and process-relational environmental thinkers (some of whom, like Joanna Macy and Freya Matthews, identify as deep ecologists and others of whom do not). Within this broader field of critical environmental thought, Heidegger is one of many reference points, but he does constitute an important link between ecophilosophy and Continental philosophy.

Paul John Ennis: Do you share Heidegger's pessimism that an event like the moon landings represented an escalation of our homelessness on this earth? Further do you share his characterization of our age as one of Enframing or has the recent wave of green awareness made this notion out of date?

Adrian Ivakhiv: Heideggerian pessimism regarding technology, including that represented by the moon landings, is a perspective that has influenced me, and it's one I continue to consider important for any future ecological thought. Along with the writings of a more Marxian tradition of geography (such as Denis Cosgrove's work on environmental and global visuality, or Neil Smith's and Donna Haraway's work on technology, images, and nature), a Heideggerian critical philosophy of technology provides a useful counterbalance against those in the environmental movement for whom the photos of Earth from space are nothing but a positive cultural touchstone in the movement toward global environmental awareness. Thinking about the moon landings, I can't help thinking about the space race, the arms race, the Cold War, and the massive technologization of society that followed World War Two. In fact, I think of a television ad that played some years ago for Tang, the orange flavor-crystal soft drink that became popular after it was used by NASA in its Gemini flights. In the ad a couple of animated "moon men" come to Earth bearing rocks which they want to trade for Tang, the drink they apparently gained a taste for when astronauts brought it to the moon. So I think of the moon landings also as part of the commercialization of massive techno-logical enterprise – a way to get the American people on board in something much larger, and much less salutary, than the "one small step for man" that Neil Armstrong famously referred to. But I also think of how the photographs have affected people on a deep and not only conscious level, making it that much more possible for us to think of humanity as a single entity, and of the earth as a single interconnected set of living processes. Ecologists in the 1950s and 1960s had tried to convey this kind of idea using energy flow diagrams that looked like electrical circuit diagrams, but it wasn't until an image of the blue orb floating in black space became visible that many people arrived at that idea on a visceral level. I think both of these perspectives – the optimistic and the pessimistic, if you will – are valid and that the truth, if there be such a thing, is one that holds them in a relationship of tension, a sort of Zen koan for our times.

One of the concepts I've worked with in my writing on religion is "double-faith," which is how some historians describe the syncretistic fusion of Christian and pagan elements found in traditional East European folk religion, and I think that's an appropriate way to conceptualize people's relationship to science, religion, and environmentalism today – all of them claim, and obtain, people's faith in different ways. Something can be both "good" and "bad" at once, both enabling and constraining, because it's not a static piece of the world, but rather is part of a series of processes in which we're implicated and in which we can be oriented this way or that way. I'm more interested in the processes by which people take up images and ideas, like the moon-shot. In that sense I'm a Deleuzian and a Whiteheadian – I see reality as process-relational, so it's more important to think about how we take up and work with the possibilities of a given image or concept than it is to become wedded to a single explanation that will account for things once and for all. Bakhtin's emphasis on the dialogical nature of meanings may be useful here as well. In a Bakhtinian sense, there'd be no Derrida, no Foucault, and perhaps no deep ecology without Heidegger and the concatenation of other ideas and developments that made them possible. Heidegger opened up a lot of possibilities for thinking about technology, but in a world that is post-Heidegger, post-McLuhan, and soon to be post-Latour, we need more nuance than his thinking alone provides.

As for the recent wave of green awareness, my sense is that a lot of environmentalists are fairly pragmatic, and that it's widely recognized that new technologies, or eco-technologies, are not only possible but are necessary in any shift toward a more ecologically sustainable society. If technology were a single entity, it might be correct to say that it "enframes" the world. But I think it's more accurate and more helpful to say that technology is multiple – that there are potentially as many technologies, or at least ways of connecting tools to humans to other entities, as there are objects in the world. This is in line with a Latourian understanding of technology – which doesn't mean that technology is "neutral" and only becomes value-laden when we subject it to particular uses (that's the kind of social construc- tionist perspective Latour disavows) but, rather, that techno- logical systems, and the ways we and the world become incorpo- rated into "networks" or "collectives" that include technological mediators, are much more hybrid, variable, and unpredictable than a strictly Heideggerian approach allows for. The moon-shot, for instance, wasn't intended to give people a sense of global ecological relatedness; it was intended to win the space race, to put the American flag on the moon, and to excite American voters so as to keep the money flowing for other technological projects. That it did the former, too, tells us something about the technology and about the ontological, or at least epistemological, opening that it made possible. So in a sense, the moon-shot got out of control of the goals which it was intended to meet. That makes it more interesting than a simple reaction of "gosh, we weren't even meant to be up in the stratosphere, let alone on the moon." But then that reaction gets replaced by another one – "gosh, isn't the Earth beautiful" – and that one starts to sink into the sediment of common sense, at which point the pessimist's interpretation becomes useful again.

Paul John Ennis: Can you tell us a little bit about the relationship between environmentalism and philosophy more generally? Do you think Continental philosophy and environmentalism are natural allies in that they both, at a basic root level, oppose Cartesian metaphysics? I think it would be fair to state that you oppose anthropocentrism. Does this mean that the early existential Analytic of Heidegger's Being and Time *does not go far enough?*

Adrian Ivakhiv: The relationship between environmentalism and philosophy is complex, and a great deal depends on how we define each of the terms. If philosophy is what's taught in university philosophy departments, then environmentalism figures into it only as a marginal side topic, where philosophical or ethical theories get applied to "current problems," in this case environmental problems. Of all environmental/philosophical hybrids, the field of environmental ethics is the most developed and widespread; it has its own journals, courses in most universities, and so on. Environmental philosophy has more recently been getting institutionalized in this way as well. But if what we mean by philosophy is the practice of philosophizing – thinking through and making sense of things in a rigorous way – then the relationship is much more robust and pervasive. Environmental thought or "eco-theory" has gone on for as long as there has been an environmental movement – at least since the 1960s, but conceivably much further back (e.g. the conservationism of the late 19th century), with critical contributions coming from historians (like Lynn White Jr.), geographers (from Humboldt and George Perkins Marsh to David Harvey), social scientists, biologists, educators, theologians, and others.

But "environmentalism" can also be traced, in some sense, through the entire history of human relations with the nonhuman world, including philosophical deliberations over that relationship. An important way in which students encounter this environment-philosophy connection is through anthologies and overviews of "ideas of nature" or of the relationship between people and nature, as found in popular writers like Jared Diamond (*Collapse*), Clive Ponting (*Green History of the World*), and others. These are typically superficial and focus too much on ideas (though Diamond manages to avoid that), but they can be useful when appropriately approached. I teach a course called "Nature and Culture," which is supposed to provide exactly that kind of big-picture background, and which raises all sorts of challenges in terms of how to avoid the typical pitfalls and instead aim for a kind of critical thinking, interdisciplinary, paradigm recognizing, comfortable-with-complexity form of thought that students rarely want to get, but which is essential for environmental scholarship of any kind. But conceived more strictly – with "environmentalism" being the mainstream environmental movement of the last 40 years, and Continental philosophy being the left branch, so to speak, of academic philosophy – I do think that the two could be natural allies, though this hasn't always been seen as such. The so-called "nature wars" of the 1990s, emanating from the "science wars" and the fallout from Bill Cronon's cultural constructivist argument about wilderness that appeared in the New York Times Magazine, showed that there was a lot of resentment among environmental academics (and many non-academics) toward their cultural and political theory brethren for the ways the latter seem to get caught up in self-important intellectual navel-gazing, e.g., terminological innovation based on the latest fads from France, and so on, rather than providing useful ways of resolving real-world problems, which were rightly thought of as reaching a point of some urgency. Fortunately, I think that moment has passed, partly because the sort of "high social constructivism" that was so prominent then has dissipated somewhat (with all manner of post-constructivist things arising in social and cultural theory, and now in Continental philosophy, as with speculative realism), and partly because of some political realignments in the US, including the opening up of a more promising frontier for environmentalism.

The opposition to Cartesian metaphysics seemed an obvious point of alliance for me when I was starting out on my doctoral work at the beginning of the 1990s, and it was both a source of frustration that a lot of other people didn't see that, and a point of identity for me and others to take it on as our "thing." But I also suspect that the opposition of Cartesianism and anti-Cartesianism has also been dissipating, partly due to the work of people in a range of fields, from philosophy to cognitive science, who have gone beyond any strict Cartesianism. I try to situate my own work within this fertile and overlapping terrain of post-constructivist discourses, where the ideas of philosophers (like Deleuze, Whitehead, and the speculative realists) kick up against ideas from science studies (Latour, Haraway and the feminist technoscience folks), "new" scientific thinking (such as the emergent/complex systems theorists like Prigogine and Kaufmann, the third-wave cognitivism of Franceso Varela and others, etc.), the poststructural and materialist traditions in social and cultural theory, the burgeoning critical animal studies field, and so on. Within all that, Cartesianism seems to be less of a monolithic enemy now and more of a ghost.

Regarding anthropocentrism, the anthropocentrism I oppose is the kind that understands humans to be the center of the moral universe or the top of the chain of being. I don't particularly feel that humans need to be "demoted" – that's already been done, in any case, by Copernicus, Darwin, Freud, and Nietzsche (whose work we could gain much more from than many people have, but which I think has gradually been internalized over time). Rather I would want us to learn a more "decentered" view that sees relationships, including relations between people but crucially also relations between humans and nonhumans, as central. Focusing on relational process raises questions of obligation, care, coexistence, and the capacity for living together and constructing viable social-natural collectives – questions of "cosmopolitics," to use Latour's and Isabelle Stengers' evocative term. Heidegger's earlier work, while it retained a mild form of anthropocentrism, enabled a blurring of the boundaries between self and world, and between mind and body, that has been very useful. Its uptake by other phenomenologists and hermeneuticists, from Merleau-Ponty to their many Continentalist followers like Edward Casey, John Caputo, John Sallis, Alphonso Lingis, John Llewellyn, and others, and even by social philosophers like Charles Taylor, and cognitivist theorists like Varela, Evan Thompson, and Michael Wheeler, has been very helpful for reorienting our understanding of ourselves toward a more relational, embodied and embedded one.

I think of Heidegger's later work as providing a set of possibilities for us to work with once we pass through the post-Cartesian door that his early work opened up. In other words, once it becomes clear to me that I am not a mind-monad coming to know a world rationally and objectively, but that I am a "there-being" (*Da-sein*) finding myself always already in the midst of situations of care and concern ("I care, therefore I am" rather than "I think, therefore I am"), the question then becomes one of "worlding": What kind of a world is this in which I find myself? How do we continually constitute the world as it is, and how might we do it differently? What's the role of our technologies, our arts and poetry, our languaging practices, in co-constituting the world in this particular way, or in another way? Derrida described Heidegger's four-fold as a beautiful postcard, but a metaphysical postcard nonetheless. I don't reject the need to speculate metaphysically and to come up with ontological descriptions of the world; in fact, I think we could do much more of that, and be creative, open and pluralistic about it. I see Heidegger's later work as providing an important contribution to that, but it's not the end of the line.

Paul John Ennis: What has environmental thinking made of object-oriented philosophy or speculative realism? Do you think the two can learn from each other?

Adrian Ivakhiv: I haven't seen much uptake yet of object-oriented philosophy or speculative realism by environmental thinkers – other than a smattering of bloggers – but I'm sure it's beginning to happen, especially among grad students tuning into the philosophical blogosphere. Of the thinkers most influential in object-oriented philosophy/speculative realism circles (besides Heidegger), it's been Latour and Deleuze who have been making the greatest impact in environmental theory. Among those who do green cultural studies, "social nature" theory (geographers like Bruce Braun, Noel Castree, Sarah Whatmore, and Steve Hinchliffe), or eco-religious studies (including theorists of animism and neopaganism like Graham Harvey), Latour has long been embraced for the way actor-network theory opens up possibilities for reconceptualizing human-nature and human-animal relations. I'm sure that Latour's uptake by philosophers like Harman will be welcomed as it filters through into the more applied forms of theorizing that take place in the social and environmental fields. (I wonder, though, why Latour's gotten so much attention by speculative realists while Haraway, who's been much more engaged in environmental and animal issues, hasn't). Gradually Žižek, Agamben, Badiou, Ranciere, and others have been taken up as well – which probably sounds pretty out-of-date to cutting-edge philosophers like the speculative realists, but environmental theory has been wrapped up in its own set of concerns, with the "big" schools of thought like ecocentrism, feminism, Marxism, anarchism, pan-indigenism, postcolonialism and Third Worldism, eco-holism, discourse theory, eco-modernization, et al. still the dominant voices. For speculative realism to have a marked influence on environmental thinking, it will need to make its case more obviously relevant to environmental practice. Part of that relevance, though, is the return of an understanding that ontology matters, and that's happening as Continentalist environmental philosophers shift out of a phenomenological, Merleau-Pontian/Heidegerian interest in perception towards a greater engagement with politics and technology – which they are doing via Deleuze and a growing interest in complexity theory (DeLanda and Prigogine), enactive cognitivism, and the like.

I'm still waiting to see if speculative realism will coalesce into something more unified or if it will fragment and dissipate. I'm not sure yet if the term means anything more than work that's speculatively ontological (in the sense that Deleuze's and Whitehead's work was) and non-anthropocentric (which can also be said of both of them). But as long as it helps revitalize philosophers' ability to deal with the "things of the world" again, and in new ways, I'm all for it, and I hope other environmental thinkers will watch it evolve and, even better, participate in it.

Paul John Ennis: I've written before about Arne Naess and Martin Heidegger as two thinkers who not only reached the occasional similar conclusions, but actually lived similar lifestyles. Yet there seems to be a major difference at the level of politics. Do you think Heidegger is ultimately tainted for environmentalism and deep ecology due to his association with National Socialism?

Adrian Ivakhiv: That's an interesting point about the similarities in the ways these two thinkers lived their lives, and I think that a lot of deep ecologists have styled themselves in similar ways – love of mountains, simple living, the backwoods wandering aesthetic, etc. Though judging by my students, love of the mountains today goes along best with snowboarding, the northern Appalachian equivalent of surfing – it's still about feeling a kind of oneness with nature, though a high-speed one, as my friend Bron Taylor documents in his recent book on *Dark Green Religion*. From what I know, Naess in person was a more likeable character than Heidegger, and perhaps that fact, along with the circumstances of their lives – Heidegger's being well positioned to take himself rather seriously in 1930s Germany, a Germany in which academic one-upmanship was more solidly established than in 1960s-70s Norway – could go some way towards accounting for the differences in their political positions. Heidegger's Nazi episode will always be something Heideggerians need to work out for themselves, since it was in retrospect such a bad move, and it's important to ask what's missing in his philosophy that made it possible for him to think that Nazism could be good, or at least that it might be redeemed through his own philosophical leadership. If we needed heroes, then I don't think environmentalists, or environmental thinkers, will find one in Heidegger. Naess, the philosopher-mountaineer, Gandhian and Norwegian Green Party activist, and good conversationalist, provides a more attractive figure to idolize. But philosophers shouldn't look for heroes; they should look for useful ideas to work with, and Heidegger had plenty of those.

Environmental activists will find their heroes elsewhere.

Paul John Ennis: Can you tell us a little bit about what you are currently working on?

Adrian Ivakhiv: I'm writing a book entitled *Ecologies of the Moving Image: Cinema, Affect, and Nature* (for Wilfrid Laurier University Press's Environmental Humanities series), in which I develop a notion of cinema as "world-disclosing" in terms of the "three ecologies" Felix Guattari described as making up relational ontology of the world (the social, the material, and the "mental" or perceptual). The goal is to get outside the dualistic frame where humans are "subjects" and everything else is "object," and instead to get at the level where a medium such as film contributes to the ways in which subjectivity and objecthood are mutually constituted within the same acts, events, and experiences. I'm also trying to wrap up an earlier, messier work of eco-cultural theory that is essentially about territorialization and its many enchantments, with case studies from work I've done over the years, including on art exhibitions, music festivals, and quasi-religious movements in Eastern Europe, maritime eastern Canada, and the US Southwest. And I'm developing a third project that theorizes the religion/secularism duality from a perspective of "radical immanence" or "immanent naturalism," as William Connolly calls it. Connolly has been instrumental in bringing Continental philosophy, Deleuze, neuroscience, and other SR-relevant themes into political theory. This brings me back to some of the more ethnographic work I had done on pilgrimage and "place-practices" in my doctoral work and first book (*Claiming Sacred Ground*), but allows me to more clearly work out the particular fusion of Latourian, Deleuzian, Heideggerian, Buddhist and process-relational thought that I've been grappling with since then.

Paul John Ennis: If you had the chance to give your younger self advice on graduate school what would it be?

Adrian Ivakhiv: I had been out of school for a couple of years pursuing various arts-related projects before I made the decision, very hesitantly, to return to academe for graduate study. At the time, I had been involved in some activist projects with local anarchist collectives, environmental initiatives, and East European solidarity work – this was the mid-1980s when the Soviet Union was opening up rapidly. And when the Chernobyl accident happened, I felt a need, oddly enough, to theorize better and more effectively, to think about the links between environmental practice, worldview (socialist, capitalist, and their alternatives), and different means of communicating the links between them. So I did a Master's in Environmental Studies at one of the most interdisciplinary places where one could do that, at York University in Canada, working with the best environmental thinkers I could find: Neil Evernden, who had just authored *The Natural Alien*, which brought Merleau-Ponty and Heidegger to environmental issues in a way that seemed exciting; John Livingston, who had created the television program *The Nature of Things* (later hosted by David Suzuki) and whose teaching really set my mind on fire; and Alejandro Rojas, who had been the youngest member of the Salvador Allende government in Chile, and who had moved from a red to a green position politically and philosophically, for reasons that made a lot of sense to me. My doctoral studies grew directly out of my Master's and were even more transdisciplinary: my advisor, Jody Berland, was a sociologist of media and environment, and my committee included a philosopher, a scholar of East Asian and indigenous religion, two geographers (one of them trained in European political theory), and an anthropologist.

The virtues of being trained as an interdisciplinarian is that one learns to speak more than one academic language and to bridge the differences between them, and between academe and the real world. The main disadvantage is that disciplines prefer not to recognize you as one of them. In some, such as geography (which claims environmental studies for itself), this isn't as big a deal as in, say, philosophy, where to get hired, at the very least you need a Ph.D. in philosophy, if not in the specific kind of philosophy they're looking for (and probably not Continental). So my teaching appointments and even job interviews have tended to be in interdisciplinary programs – environmental studies, science and technology studies, global studies. The good thing, for young scholars with inter- or anti-disciplinary leanings, is that interdisciplinary and transdisciplinary work (and I won't get into the differences between them) is the way of the future. The current economic crunch will most certainly put greater pressure on the traditional structure of disciplines, and will lead to the creation of bolder new programs that aim to come to grips with the problems of our time: global climate change, depletion of resources, ethnic and territorial violence, global wealth disparities, and the many interrelationships between these. Philosophy departments will continue to plod along as they have, but there won't be as many of them, and even philosophers will have to work together with others for their work to have much impact. So I would urge any aspiring grad student who feels confined within a single discipline to seek out a good place where interdisciplinarity is actually cultivated and not just stumbled upon, and then to make that part of your identity. But there aren't yet many places that do that well, so you may need to combine a disciplinary degree with a more interdisciplinary one. The future is in the hands of those who know how to work on shifting and unstable grounds.

Paul John Ennis: What, in your opinion, is the future of post-Continental philosophy?

Adrian Ivakhiv: Continental philosophy has been a good gauge of the changing horizons of a rapidly transforming society.

Language, interpretation, embodiment, technology, religious and cultural pluralism, sexuality, identity and otherness – all of these have seen rapid changes in a globalizing context. And now ecology, materiality, and the moral conundrums associated with biotechnologies and biopolitics, food and human-animal relations, and the like, will all provide further fuel for philosophical innovation. My sense is that a lot of Continental philosophy, especially in North America, has done a good job cultivating an esoteric discourse that no one outside its ranks understands or cares to understand, so it's been very refreshing to see folks like Graham Harman and some of the others you're interviewing here, as well as Žižek, Hardt and Negri, and Jodi Dean, among others, find a more resonant language as well as extra-disciplinary venues for their work. In an increasingly global context, I'm not sure if either "Continental philosophy" or "Analytical philosophy" have much of a future except as carriers of certain legacies; they're carry-overs from a time when philosophy seemed exclusive to the North Atlantic world. In a globally mediated, technologically shaped world of shifting and intersecting biocultural contexts, philosophy will have to be more hybrid, viral, and shapeshifting if it's to remain relevant and efficacious as a motivating and inspirational source for cosmopolitical world-making – which, to my mind, is what lies ahead of us. Post-Continental philosophy will have to also be post-Analytical, post-feminist, post-Marxist, post-postcolonial, post-constructivist, somehow culturally engaged, and if not post- then at least not pre-ecological. I see glimpses of that in the work of Manuel DeLanda, Reza Negarestani, Susan Buck-Morss, Arturo Escobar, Stefan Helmreich, William Connolly, Isabelle Stengers, and a lot of other people; but there's plenty of work ahead of us. I think the one piece of advice I would leave any aspiring philosopher today is not to read just philosophy. But does anyone still do that nowadays?

Interview with Lee Braver

Paul John Ennis: You were personally involved in an online reading group for your book A Thing of This World. *Was this exercise a success and do you think online reading groups have anything to tell us about the emerging blog culture associated with many contemporary philosophical movements?*

Lee Braver: It has certainly been a success in raising the book's profile and getting feedback from readers. Keep in mind that several hundred thousand books in English are published each year, so bringing titles to the attention of those who may be interested in them presents a real problem. Our training in graduate school, by its very nature, gives us a distorted picture of the profession: we study with prominent scholars, who get invited to speak all over the world and whose writings are widely discussed and reviewed. By default, this experience moulds our impression of the profession, but it represents a highly atypical, tiny minority. The vast majority of Ph.D.'s, if they get jobs at all, work at teaching schools and, if they publish, their publications sink beneath the surface with barely a ripple. This has been perhaps my greatest surprise since I've started publishing, how little attention one's work receives, or at least that one is aware of. My expectations were, naturally, formed by what I read: the important works that everyone reads and discusses and writes about. Getting my book onto people's radar and seeing people engage with it has been very gratifying, and I feel fortunate for the opportunity.

I really don't have much to say about the medium of blogging, since I'm not very active in it. I'm astonished at how assiduously people write and read them; I find both processes very time-consuming. Of course, it pays dividends in allowing for far more conversation than would otherwise be available to most people, especially those stranded in small departments (another common fate filtered out by the blinders of grad school). If Gadamer is right about the importance of dialogue to thought, and I think he is, blogs represent a tremendous opening up of opportunities. I've been a little surprised — again, perhaps naively — at the gaps of civility, patience, informed objections, and charity that occur rather regularly in internet discussions. Combined with anonymity, the immediacy of posting seems to encourage some of our baser intellectual instincts: being dismissive, closed-minded, waiting for your turn to talk rather than genuinely listening. Gadamer's views on hermeneutic humility should guide us here.

Paul John Ennis: You've written an excellent reader's guide to Heidegger's Later Writings. *Why do you think the later Heidegger is becoming so popular and do you think there is still room for the early writings?*

Lee Braver: Personally, I'm surprised that later Heidegger isn't more influential. The narrative I trace in *A Thing of This World: A History of Continental Anti-Realism* tries to show why Heidegger deserves a dominant place in the pantheon by plotting his innovations with precision. *Being and Time* is unquestionably a masterpiece and I can't imagine it disappearing from the canon, but it is a flawed and incomplete masterpiece. In addition to an apparently ahistorical analysis of *Dasein*'s essential structure, it retains an existentialist voluntarism that I find unsatisfying and even a bit crude. Death, anxiety, and conscience allow us to step back and "choose to choose," in Kierkegaardian language.

I find the later works more important and innovative, offering intellectual riches we have barely begun to explore and exploit. They contain exhilarating and revelatory "phenomenological" descriptions, as well as some of the most insightful and fascinating philosophical analyses I've ever come across. Just to take the example of voluntarism, I've written about how his later conception of agency offers a rigorously argued model that escapes the dead-ends of free will and determinism.

Two reasons for the early work's comparative popularity are that 1) *Being and Time* is more accessible, especially given the number of figures one can use to triangulate it (Kant, Husserl, Kierkegaard, Dilthey), and 2) it plays the helpful role of the *magnum opus*. The later work's lack of a single work that can impart the gist of decades of thought creates a serious obstacle at the outset. That's why I used Krell's *Basic Writings* as the subject of my *Heidegger's Later Writings: A Reader's Guide*. Krell does a very good job of picking representative essays from across Heidegger's later career, and his collection serves quite well in lieu of a single book. Since it's the text actually used in many courses, I thought an essay-by-essay guide to it would be useful.

Paul John Ennis: As a scholar well versed in the later Heidegger what do you think he would have made of the technological beast that is the internet?

Lee Braver: Well, first, I think he would have referred to it as the she-bitch goddess of the underworld, but I can't prove it.

Bert Dreyfus has written a book on the internet which I haven't read, but which I'm sure would be illuminating on the topic. In many ways, the internet fits the culmination of technology in "cybernetics" quite nicely: it forms an enormous, frictionless, almost instantaneous circulation of knowledge, putting tremendous amounts of information at our fingertips. This facility makes us take it for granted, perhaps the most pernicious feature of technology. On the other hand, Heidegger was a great letter-writer and the internet has brought about a rebirth of correspondence. The problem, as mentioned above, is that the very speed and ease with which we can post our thoughts leads, by the logic of the essence of technology, to doing so thoughtlessly. Probably the most important line to cite here is his claim that we can use technology without letting it dominate our thinking, speaking, and acting. No technological device in itself has the power to "corrupt" us, only the essence of technology, i.e., the general way of thinking and perceiving the world that forms the ground of technology. As long as we are properly grounded, we can "safely" interact with any tool. One of the great defenses against taking things for granted is surprise, and skilful web-surfing frequently turns up utterly strange and fascinating spectacles.

Paul John Ennis: Your first book deals with both Continental and Analytic philosophy. Do you think the "divide" is somewhat artificial? What do you think Heideggerians could learn from Analytic thinkers and vice versa?

Lee Braver: In a way, all of my books have been about the divide, or at least they intentionally locate themselves in the landscape formed and deformed by it. *A Thing of This World* uses the Analytic topic of anti-realism (itself initiated by Kant, as Putnam frequently points out) as a lens to bring the development of Continental thought into focus. The goal was simultaneously to map the evolution of certain ideas across central Continental thinkers with a high degree of resolution and to make the Continental conversation accessible to those not immersed in it. *Heidegger's Later Writings: A Reader's Guide* tries to open up these very influential works to anyone not sufficiently familiar with his thought, hopefully including Analytic thinkers. The book I'm finishing now, *Standing on the Groundless Ground: A Comprehensive Study of Wittgenstein and Heidegger*, focuses on a single cross-divisional pairing to examine it in great detail.

There is a way in which the divide is artificial, and a way it is not. I think there are substantive differences in the way Continental and Analytic thinkers generally approach issues (of course, with plenty of exceptions), some of which I have tried to trace. It is the lack of communication that I find both unnecessary and unfortunate. Perhaps we could say that it's a meaningful distinction, but an artificial division. As philosophers, we are supposed to be arguing with each other, not ignoring each other. We have a lot to learn from each other — especially in light of our different approaches — though I don't think one can simply list particular ideas that one branch should adopt from the other. It's more a matter of Gadamer's notion that we only see our own taken-for-granted prejudices when we take seriously those who lack them. In this way, the differences should be seen as provocative and productive rather than preventative. This kind of dialogue does require a considerable amount of preparation, some of which I have tried to do (I also engage in the dialogue itself, e.g., giving a Heideggerian response to Davidson's denial of conceptual schemes, a Derridean deconstruction of Frege, etc.). I suspect that the lack of background knowledge represents the primary obstacle to fruitful interaction. My books try to prepare the ground by constructing a common vocabulary and demonstrating the existence of common topics.

Paul John Ennis: There has been a lot of discussion about the speculative realist movement. Your first book attempts to show how the two big traditions of Analytic and Continental philosophy are more or less concerned with the problems of realism/anti-realism, albeit from their respective trenches: what do you make of speculative realism?

Lee Braver: I'm just starting to get a sense of speculative realism; I want to undertake a more serious study of it, along with Deleuze, once I'm done with my present project. When I first encountered it – in Graham Harman's work on Heidegger – I didn't know what to make of it. I was firmly entrenched in anti-realism and couldn't conceive of a sophisticated realism; it seemed to me that any realism would have to ignore all the ideas generated in Kant's wake. So much realism amounts to Johnsonian rock-kicking, or *ad hominem* attacks on the intelligence of anyone lacking a sufficiently robust realism. I am quite intrigued by the movement. The first part of

Meillassoux's *After Finitude* loosened my unquestioning allegiance to anti-realism, though it didn't quite convince me to jump ship.

Paul John Ennis: Now that you've tackled a whole range of thinkers and even attempted to straddle the divide between the two traditions what are you planning to take on next?

Lee Braver: Surprisingly, I've stuck to the plan announced in *A Thing of This World*. I'm almost finished with the book on Heidegger and Wittgenstein. I'm still carrying on the project of dialogue across the divide but I've exchanged the breadth of *A Thing* for a deeper and more focused analysis. This book has the regulative (not constitutive!) ideal of being the last book that ever needs to be written on this pairing; I examine and bring into dialogue both thinkers" early and later works across their most central topics. It's simply astonishing how much agreement there is between the greatest philosopher of each tradition.

Paul John Ennis: If you had the chance to give your younger self advice on graduate school what would it be?

Lee Braver: I'm tempted to tell him not to go; there are so many chances to end up in unsatisfying situations that I sometimes get retrospective vertigo just thinking about my own fate. While it's true that I can't imagine myself doing anything else (I often wonder how normal people manage to get up in the morning, knowing what monotony faces them), that may very well be due to an insufficiently robust imagination rather than deep self-knowledge. I think of the line from *New York Stories* where an apprentice of an established painter wants to know if he thinks she's any good, so that she can quit if she isn't. He tells her, "if you can quit, you should."

One point that has only slowly dawned on me is the importance of relationships for one's career. I started with a naive view of academia as a true meritocracy where quality automatically rises to the top. This frequently happens in the long run, but in the short run a tremendous amount depends on who you know. Having a dissertation chair that's well-connected and committed to using her connections on your behalf can make an enormous difference in your professional fate. Opportunities to present and publish often travel along paths worn by friendship and familiarity. Another factor that's far larger than I ever imagined is plain luck.

I would also want to straighten him out on research. I initially subscribed to the idea that publications were not very significant, since most get a quick skim by a handful of scholars before settling into a permanent, undisturbed slumber on a dusty shelf. What I didn't realize was the impact of writing on the writer. When I write, I'm generally trying to explain these issues to myself, to think them through carefully rather than just spilling fully formed ideas onto the page. Certainly, we're obligated to put tremendous effort into making these thoughts accessible to readers; one must be a good host, after all. But, necessarily, one's first audience is always oneself. And I've learned a great deal from my work.

Here's one actual piece of advice: if you read something that impresses or intrigues you, drop the author a line. Email is a godsend for academia. Most scholars are very friendly, even grateful to know that someone's reading their work and, from a self-interested point of view, these contacts can be surprisingly valuable to one's career. The worst that can happen? No response.

Paul John Ennis: What, in your opinion, is the future of post-Continental philosophy?

Lee Braver: As you can imagine from my scholarly focus, I find it hard to imagine that the Analytic-Continental divide will continue much longer, at least in its present form. Many of its most doctrinaire adherents are dying off (an essential step in paradigm shift, according to Kuhn) and plenty of younger philosophers have little invested in it. The mere fact of specialization means that we must pass over the vast majority of what's out there, but walling off a whole tradition, intentionally rendering oneself incapable of grasping the basic ideas of potential interlocutors, will hopefully come to be as obsolete as medicinal leeches.

Contemporary culture has eliminated both the concept of the public and the figure of the intellectual. Former public spaces – both physical and cultural – are now either derelict or colonized by advertising. A cretinous anti-intellectualism presides, cheerled by expensively educated hacks in the pay of multinational corporations who reassure their bored readers that there is no need to rouse themselves from their interpassive stupor. The informal censorship internalized and propagated by the cultural workers of late capitalism generates a banal conformity that the propaganda chiefs of Stalinism could only ever have dreamt of imposing. Zer0 Books knows that another kind of discourse – intellectual without being academic, popular without being populist – is not only possible: it is already flourishing, in the regions beyond the striplit malls of so-called mass media and the neurotically bureaucratic halls of the academy. Zer0 is committed to the idea of publishing as a making public of the intellectual. It is convinced that in the unthinking, blandly consensual culture in which we live, critical and engaged theoretical reflection is more important than ever before.